1985

THE QUESTION OF PLAY

Drew A. Hyland

UNIVERSITY
PRESS OF
AMERICA

LANHAM • NEW YORK • LONDON

Copyright © 1984 by

University Press of America,™ Inc.

4720 Boston Way
Lanham, MD 20706

3 Henrietta Street
London WC2E 8LU England

Library of Congress Cataloging in Publication Data

Hyland, Drew A.
    The question of play.

    Bibliography: p.
    Includes index.
    1. Play (Philosophy) I. Title.
B105.P54H94   1984   128   84–8460
ISBN 0–8191–4005–8 (alk. paper)
ISBN 0–8191–4006–6 (pbk. : alk. paper)

All University Press of America books are produced on acid-free
paper which exceeds the minimum standards set by the National
Historical Publications and Records Commission.

For my brother, Art, my first play-mate,

and, as always, for Anne, Christopher, and Craig.

The soul is its own <u>logos</u>, which
increases itself.

Heraclitus, Fragment 115

Table of Contents

Prelude

This book has arisen out of a necessity of thought whose personal basis I shall try to explain in the Introduction. Still, there are more than ample scholarly reasons for writing a book on play. As everyone who begins to take this important topic seriously knows all too well, there is a long-standing and totally unjustified academic prejudice against play which insists that it is not a topic for serious thought. As a result, relatively few thinkers have turned attention on the topic, and there has been a dearth of thoughtful works on play which is only recently beginning to be overcome. My hope is that the present book will be a contribution to that overcoming.

The structure of the book is fairly simple but perhaps deserves some explanation. The first three chapters take up three dominant standpoints in the light of which play is often considered (I speak of "standpoints" rather than "methodologies" because there is in my view all too much dispute over the latter notion within each standpoint). I call these standpoints, speaking loosely, the sociological, psychological, and historical, respectively. I shall be offering a critique of these standpoints in the Kantian sense; I shall try to set out initially what sorts of insights and issues concerning play each standpoint can reveal, but also set out the limitations or boundaries of each, and so what each conceals in what it reveals. If I am successful, these considerations will lead ineluctibly to the philosophic standpoint, perhaps because all thinking leads ineluctibly to this standpoint once one starts on the way. In Part II, then, I shall venture my own conception of what I call the stance of play. From this, much, for me at least, follows, and so in Part III, after a chapter devoted to the most significant alternative conceptions of play, I take up a variety of specific topics which are evidently related to play, and see how things stand with them in the light of my view. The book will have no formal conclusion because the logic of play, like the logic of the soul to which Heraclitus alludes in the aphorism with which I begin, demands that there be none. Nevertheless, as I hope to show, play, again like the soul, has a logos which increases itself.

I played for a long while with a variety of formats for the book which would be manifestly "playful": a dialogue, a correspondence between two fictional characters, a journal. I finally decided on this relatively orthodox format on the grounds that, if I am successful, the book itself will be an exhibition of the deeper sense of playfulness which is set out herein.

I wish to express my thanks to the many students who have taken my course, "Philosophy of Sport" at Trinity College. Their questions, contributions, and criticisms regularly inform this book. I owe special thanks to David Roochnik, who thinks as intensely as he plays.

Finally and most of all, thanks to my family, Anne, Christopher, and Craig, who live out with me the intimacy of play and love.

Introduction

There is a widespread misconception concerning the efficacy of thinking about certain topics which runs approximately as follows: some things in life -- love, art, play, for example -- cannot be reflected upon adequately. They must be experienced, and the sure sign that one has truly experienced them is the recognition of the utter irrelevance of further efforts to think about them. Love, or art, or play, "can´t be explained". Indeed, the very effort to do so is suspicious; it suggests a certain weakness of experience, that one has not "really lived" the experience in question. "Those who can´t do it think about it" (or "teach it", or "coach it" or "write about it"). This prejudice culminates in the stereotype of the "ivory tower egg-head" who thinks, writes or teaches out of a paucity of real living in what is curiously called "the real world".

I begin this book not merely by denying this thesis but by affirming an opposite view. Reflection, I want to suggest, is occasioned not by weakness of experience but by its excess. What are those experiences upon which we do not need to reflect, which do not demand reflection? Precisely those experiences which are sufficiently weak that we can "let them be". They are sufficiently weak that they could be said to exhaust themselves and their significance in the immediate experience. For example, I have never reflected on the significance of brushing my teeth. Why not? Because there is nothing in the experience of teethbrushing (for me at least!) which is sufficiently powerful that it demands preservation in thought, or sufficiently problematic, troubling, puzzling, that it occasions thought. It is what I call a weak experience, and the sure sign of its weakness is that it has never occurred to me to think about it. But there are other experiences which do occasion or even demand reflection, which are too powerful to let alone, which do not exhaust themselves in the immediacy of the experience. They are, to use Sartre´s apt term, de trop, too much. They can be de trop negatively; such experiences as these are what the Continental European tradition has centered upon as the core experiences of authenticity and the core occasions for reflection: Angst, Dread, the Absurd, Death, Nausea. But experiences can also be too powerful positively, as the experience of love, or art, friendship, peacefulness, or joy. In either case, the initial point is that reflection upon these themes is demanded not out of a weakness of experience but out of strength; they are "too much" to leave alone. They must be preserved, mulled over, clarified, even if never resolved. To make the point once more, if, after the experience of death, or of love, one is not moved to thought, that testifies to a weak experience thereof indeed. "Those who don't need to think about it didn't truly experience it". Reflection, the word I have used for this thinking, is thus not an abstracting or standing back from experience but more like facing up to and responding to an experience that demands preservation.

Play has been such a de trop experience for me, and I shall presently indicate some of the reasons why. But first, I want to qualify the previous remarks by affirming that I understand that and why thinking on such topics has received a bad name. As a look at some of the current literature on play will reveal, the wrong kind of thinking has too often been done. To clarify my point, note that in speaking of the reflection demanded by these de trop experiences, I spoke of the necessity of "preserving", "mulling over", and "clarifying" them, but not of "resolving" them. Moreover, I earlier admitted the impossibility of "explaining" them. I must try, then, to give some sense of the difference between that thought -- I have used the terms "reflection" or "reflective clarification" -- which preserves, mulls over, and clarifies, and that thought which explains and resolves. The real exhibition of the difference, of course, must be in the way this book, hopefully, will be a manifestation of the former.

In Plato's dialogue, Phaedrus, Socrates makes the pregnant remark that he has always been "a lover of divisions and collections" (Phaedrus 266b). I have always taken this to be a pointer to understanding the kind of thinking Socrates does. By "divisions" I take him to mean what we today call "analytical" thinking, that thinking which distinguishes into kinds or sub-species, which makes subtle distinctions, which breaks down a complex argument or concept into its components. This is surely the kind of thinking at which the followers of so-called "analytic philosophy", which has until recently dominated the English-speaking world, excel. But its critics argue that the failure of analytic philosophy is that it only, or at least too exclusively, analyzes. In Socrates´ metaphor, it forgets that the philosopher must be a lover of divisions <u>and</u> collections.

At this point we can already see one kind of inadequate thinking all too prevalent in contemporary writing on play: what we might call "mere" analysis. Too many books and especially too many articles indulge predominantly in this mode of thinking. But what is the inadequacy here? Surely not that it is wrong to draw careful distinctions, to analyze complex issues and arguments into their simpler components. Thinking that does not include such analysis almost always suffers from sloppiness, a lack of clarity, a kind of conceptual uncleanliness. The inadequacy rather lies, again, in the too exclusive application of analysis, in "mere" analysis. When this occurs, the impression is almost always given of a certain kind of abstractness, an abstractness untrue to, or at least inadequate to, our experience. For often, such distinctions as are drawn are distinctions in thought, not in experience. We do not, that is, actually experience them as distinctions. For example, suppose I draw and carefully support a distinction between "sport" and "athletics". Who experiences that distinction? The football player on the field? The runner in the Boston Marathon? (An even more famous and problematic example in philosophy is the celebrated mind/body distinction). I want to emphasize that just because our experience is sometimes not as subtle as our intellect in no way illigitimates the distinction. But it does have the effect of making such thinking a kind of abstractness, a "mere intellectual gymnastics", if, as is often done, it is left at the level of analysis.

What is needed, to return again to Socrates´ metaphor, is that we be lovers both of divisions and of collections. By "collections" I take Socrates to refer to the converse of analytic thinking, what we might call "synthetic" or "synoptic" thinking, that thinking which is especially sensitive to the unity of things and of concepts, sensitive to the way in which apparently distinct issues are tied together into a whole. One might, following Nietzsche, refer to this as a Dionysian thinking, whereas analysis would be more in the mode of the Apollinian, the <u>principium individuationis</u>. One might say that such collective thinking restores the wholeness which analytic thinking has -- however insightfully -- torn assunder.

But one must be careful not to grant a superiority to synthetic thinking (as Nietzsche himself seems to have done) in such a way as to infer the dispensibility of analytic thinking. Synthetic or synoptic thought, when it is done without the co-presence of analysis, generates its own kind of abstractness, the abstractness which blurs the real distinctions and subtleties that our experience does contain. This is the abstractness too often present in so-called eastern or mystical thought, which in its most vulgar forms asks us to find meaning in knowing that "everything is one", or that to shoot arrows with real meaning we must develop a "selfless purposelessness". Once again, I am not suggesting that such positions are false -- for all I know, selfless purposelessness is a wonderful thing -- but that by itself, without the presence of careful distinctions, such thinking almost inevitably gives the impression of abstractness. So we would seem to be faced with the danger of two kinds of abstractness in our efforts to think about our experience, the abstractness of thinking the parts only without incorporating them into a whole (the danger of analytic thinking), and the danger of thinking the whole without being sensitive to the parts (the danger of exclusively synthetic thinking). The way to avoid both, or to think the "concrete universal" in Hegel´s phrase, is to think both divisions and collections together, or so one might infer from Socrates. But I am not convinced that this is the whole of the problem.

Even if one preserves the effort to think both analytically and synthetically, there remains a danger that one will take the matter for thought in a manner untrue to its nature. One such mistake, particularly prevalent in our efforts to think about "concrete experiences" such as love, art, or play, is to treat such issues after the manner of the sciences, as "problems". Perhaps because of the dominance of the mathematical/scientific mode of thinking, we are too often inclined to this tendency. Thus in philosophy we often hear that the job of philosophy is "to solve philosophical problems", as if the issues for philosophical thought were not unlike more or less difficult mathematical equations. But such experiential issues as love, art, or play are not problems in this sense because they have no "solutions", and to orient one´s thinking on them in this direction is to misconstrue them from the beginning. This is the core of the distinction I drew earlier between a thinking that seeks to "resolve" or "explain" on the one hand, and a thinking that attempts to "preserve, mull over, and clarify" on the other. It is the latter kind of thinking which I believe is appropriate to play and which I hope to exhibit in this book, a thinking which loves "divisions and collections" and which also seeks not to solve or explain but to preserve, mull over, clarify.

I am convinced that such thinking, far from rendering abstract, weakening, or taking distance from our lived experience, enables us to deepen that experience, to appreciate it more, to preserve it more authentically and so to live it out all the more fully. A teacher of mine, Henry Bugbee, once used the metaphor of tilling the soil; the right kind of thinking tills, turns over, and at once deepens and enriches the soil of our experience. It is in this sense that I believe, with Socrates, that "the unexamined life is not worth living". For too much of contemporary philosophy, that foundational maxim would have to be altered to "the unexamined concept is not worth asserting".

One final point regarding the mode of thinking I wish here to espouse: very often, again using the mathematical sciences as our outstanding model, we presume that whatever knowledge we are able to gain will be best gained by focusing directly on the object sought. If I want to learn about the molecular constitution of water, I know of no better procedure than to concentrate my attention directly on that matter. But we must become sensitive to the fact that such is not always the case. Sometimes, at least, we come to knowledge "obliquely", in the course of some other activity or project. It is at least possible that for some knowledge the best and even the only authentic access is through this oblique acquisition. A good example of this phenomenon is the happening of self-knowledge in our play. As I shall discuss in a later chapter, it is almost uncontroversial to claim that we learn much about ourselves in our play, about our character, our fears, our abilities. But one sure way to preclude that experience is to enter into a given experience of play with the explicit intention not of playing but of gaining self-knowledge. "Today I will play basketball in order to learn about myself": not only am I unlikely to learn much, I almost certainly will fail to attain to genuine play.

We are thus faced with a curious situation: we do come to self-knowledge in experiences such as play. Perhaps we come to more and deeper self-knowledge thereby than in the more focused project, say, of seeing a psychiatrist. Yet does this not imply that we preclude this oblique knowledge immediately that we seek it, and so that if we want it, we must precisely not think about it? Not quite.

To be sure, I have argued that this oblique knowledge is not best available by focusing directly on it. But it is important to note that in the example I employed, we open ourselves to the possibility of such self-knowledge through entering the activity of playing. To generalize this, such oblique knowledge becomes available to us through entering a given activity, or even more generally, through taking a certain posture or stance toward things. We open up the possibility of self-knowledge through taking the stance of play. We can therefore prepare for such knowledge by opening ourselves to that stance, by thinking about it and practicing it. This is evidently not the same as focusing directly on the project of self-knowledge, but neither is it ignoring or forgetting about it. The kind of thinking I have in mind, then, will be in part a stance, an orientation toward things, which we can practice, preserve, nurture, and in the event of which we may attain to knowledge.

I said earlier that play has been a _de trop_ experience for me, an experience too powerful in the positive sense to leave unreflected. It may therefore be helpful to the reader to be aware of something of the experiential grounding of the book itself, and so I shall indulge in a brief excursion into autobiography -- very selective to be sure -- in the hope of giving the reader a sense of the kind of experiences which impelled this book.

I grew up in the town of Lansdowne, Pennsylvania, which is immediately adjacent to the city limits of Philadelphia. As such, many of the sociological "values" of our town derived from the city itself. In sports, this meant that basketball was king. It was fine to be a football or baseball player, but the real recognition, the real prestige and even glory, came with achievement on the basketball team. Probably for this reason (although needless to say I remember no such conscious decision) I began in seventh grade to concentrate on basketball above all things. And I mean "concentrate" in the strongest possible sense. I played basketball virtually every day of the year through high school, all day on weekends. In the winter my friends of like mind and I would get to school early to practice shooting. On weekends, when the weather made outdoor conditions unacceptable, we would travel around the city, sneaking into gymnasiums, where we would play until the custodian discovered us, whereupon we would move on to the next gym. The "Main Line" schools -- Haverford College, Villanova University, and a private school called Episcopal Academy -- had the worst security in those days, and so became more or less our home courts. Not just my time and physical energies were taken up with basketball either. It became the center of my emotional and psychological life as well. Most of the thinking I did in those early years, not to mention the fantasizing, concerned basketball. It certainly did not concern my schoolwork, about which, through high school, I remember nothing that interested me. As for girlfriends, that pretty much took care of itself as a consequence of the recognition I received from basketball, all of which seemed fine with me at the time. Thus I conformed for the most part to the stereotype of the young man who "lives for" a sport, whose deepest concerns, energies, friendships, and even values emerged in the light of my involvement with basketball. Perhaps not surprisingly, this kind of commitment yielded results, and I was by the time of high school a "star" of the team, and even though I was relatively short (5´8") my reputation began spreading throughout the county.

Meanwhile, I happened to be a very good student. As indicated above, this was certainly not because anything academic in the school inspired me. I daresay the biggest impetus was the expectation, nay demand, of my parents to do well in school if I wanted to play basketball. It is no exaggeration to say that I stayed on the honor roll largely to assure that I could continue to play basketball, although I gradually came to enjoy the reputation of being a "jock" and a "brain" as well. Perhaps the extent of my genuine commitment to my studies can best be seen by relating the incident (about which I used to boast) in my senior year when, upon the assignment of our major senior paper in English on Romeo and Juliet, I went to the local drugstore, bought the "Classic Comic", and read it rather than bother with what

struck me then as the tedium and obscurity of the
original play.

In any case, the urging from my parents to do
well in school certainly had good pragmatic
consequences, for the college that recruited me most
strongly was Princeton University, where my good
grades assured that I was easily accepted. So,
following my graduation from high school in 1957, I
followed my friend and teammate a year ahead of me,
Jim Brangan, to Princeton, to play basketball,
without, so far as I can remember, an academic thought
in my head, but utterly satisfied with my self-image
as a basketball player who "also had smarts".

The professor's comment on my first college essay
read, "The prose style of this essay cannot be
expressed in polite epithets. See me at once". So my
education began, commencing at 18 years of age. I
"discovered" books and professors, and slowly, ever so
slowly, I began to broaden my genuine concerns beyond
basketball and adolescent sexual encounters, the two
foundations of my life so far. In particular, there
were a few books -- Camus' The Stranger, Boccaccio's
Decameron, Plato's Apology and Symposium -- which for
the first time struck me as talking about something
important, and a few professors, Richard J. Browne in
particular, who brought home that importance and the
importance of ideas in general. They began to strike
me as worth thinking and talking about.

Most decisively, however, this development was
kept utterly separate from my life and being as a
basketball player, which certainly continued to center
things. I daresay the main connection that occurred
between these two spheres of my life was when a
professor would occasionally ask me for tickets to a
basketball game. No one ever suggested -- and it
certainly never occurred to me -- to think about
basketball in any sense but the technical. If I was
becoming a basketball player and a budding
intellectual, the "and" was more disjunctive than
conjunctive.

Still, certain roots were forming. On the one
hand, basketball was still the center of things,
although the developing interest in my studies,
coupled I suppose with a certain growth in my
maturity, gave that experience a less obsessive though
still very deep meaning. Certainly my self-image

xviii

continued to be centered around basketball, and why not? In my freshman year I was elected captain of the freshman team, in my sophomore year I won a varsity letter on a team that tied for the Ivy League Championship, in my junior and senior years we won the League Championship, and in my senior year we progressed as far as the quarter-finals of the NCAA Championships, farther, I believe, than any Ivy League team had gone to that time. I nurtured deep friendships with my teammates, three of whom became my roommates (a fourth was my brother, Art, who was two years behind me and later became captain of the varsity and All-Ivy League player -- I consider him the athlete of the family).

Meanwhile, a course on Plato moved me genuinely, and I began to develop a sustained commitment to a Socratic conception of philosophy. I majored in philosophy, telling myself at first that it was good preparation for law school. But by my senior year I had decided to go on to graduate school at Pennsylvania State University, which appealed to me because it emphasized the history of philosophy and had a particularly good man, Stanley Rosen, under whom I could continue my study of Greek Philosophy. The irony here -- and today the embarrassment -- is that all the while that I was becoming committed to a conception of philosophy which argued that philosophy should be an ongoing examination of one's life, that "the unexamined life was not worth living", in the midst of arguing this passionately before my intellectual peers who, under the dominance of Princeton's predominantly "analytic" philosophy department were insisting that philosophy is "the analysis of language" or "conceptual analysis", in the midst of insisting on this "existential" and personal conception of philosophy, it never occurred to me to make my own intense involvement with basketball the subject of philosophic reflection. No doubt part of the reason is that this would have been "respectable" or even acceptable neither to my professors nor to my teammates, and to say the least I was under their influence in the respective spheres.

So I went to graduate school in philosophy, my sense of self now a kind of benign schizophrenia, with two lives and life styles kept quite separate. My orientation was now different, to be sure, since my basketball career had been left behind (though only formally), and I was intent on becoming "a philosopher". Still, I continued to live and flourish partly on the reputation -- and certainly on the self-esteem -- derived from being a basketball player.

At Penn State this development continued easily. I still played basketball informally, but philosophy was becoming increasingly important. I continued to be committed to the Socratic insistence that philosophy had to do with the examination of one´s own life and so with self-knowledge, a conviction now augmented by studies of so-called "existentialist" thinkers who seemed to me to teach the same. In one course on Heidegger´s Being and Time, taught by Professor Richard Gottshalk, we were assigned the task in one of our papers of applying the Heideggerian framework to some personal experience. For the very first time, it occurred to me that I should think philosophically about my experience of basketball. There arose the occasion, and with it the felt need and desire, to draw together these so-far disparate aspects of my life and being. I wrote a paper called "Athletics and Angst: Reflections on the Philosophical Significance of Play", which in a much later version was subsequently published. When Gottshalk handed the paper back to me he looked at me and said, prophetically, "You´ll never live down the fact that you played basketball".

At the time, I assumed that one such paper was enough. I had joined together what I had formerly held assunder; I had accomplished the unity of my being as a philosopher and as a basketball player which my very conception of philosophy demanded. I could put it behind me now, and move on to the next paper on Kant. Little did I know! For I did not and could not then have appreciated that I had not just written a paper but begun a habit, the habit of turning over in my mind those aspects of my life which seemed important, my loves, my fears, my values, certainly my play, seeking to hold them together in a thoughtful unity.

So I entered upon my teaching career, intent now on preserving my reflective interest in basketball (which I now took as simply my own favorite example of "play"), although the opportunities to do so formally -- in teaching or in writing for publication -- did not easily present themselves. My first opportunity to tie my interest in play directly to my teaching came under strange and ironically negative circumstances. In 1967 I came to teach at Trinity College, in Hartford, Connecticut. Trinity is a fine school with an excellent student body. But the period of the late sixties and early seventies was hardly a time when the atmosphere on college campuses was conducive to the consideration of play. The politics of confrontation joined in a bizarre alliance with the development of the "drug culture" to produce an atmosphere which with the greatest of understatement I can call unplayful. Like many teachers, I was becoming convinced that teaching was fast becoming impossible on a campus where students were either high on drugs and/or planning the next sit-in. In an almost desparate effort to find a situation where teaching and learning -- thinking -- would be possible, I developed a scheme whereby a group of students, instead of taking four or five different courses from different teachers, would study one sustained project under my direction for the semester. This freed us from the necessity of staying on campus, which is what I wanted. I proposed to take the students with my family to the mountains of Vermont for the winter term, where we would pursue a broadly construed program of study on the relationship between human being and nature, and human being and play. An imaginative and sympathetic Dean of the Faculty, Robert Fuller, and the President of the College, Theodore Lockwood, gave their nihil obstat if not their imprimatur, and off we went to Vermont for the first of three such programs which I conducted in the ensuing years. The students quickly labeled the program "Skiing and Being", and it proved the most successful educational project in which I have ever participated. I was able there to develop more fully and thematically my interest in play and its appeal to human being, and began to develop some of the ideas which inform the present book.

Two other teaching experiences need to be mentioned as background for the writing of this book. The first is my effort to develop a course at Trinity called "Philosophy of Sport". This began when two students, David Roochnik and Nat Williams, asked me to offer them a tutorial on the topic. I did, and out of it came the course, which I first offered in 1974. It was in this course that I have been called upon to formulate more fully the material that I present in this book. Needless to say, the students in all these courses have been invaluable, helping me, through questions, criticisms, and positive suggestions of their own, to develop my standpoint more adequately.

The second teaching experience has been my involvement helping to coach the women´s basketball team at Trinity during the early years of co-education at Trinity in the seventies. This experience has deepened my appreciation of a variety of themes which had long been with me concerning play. I came to understand, first, that coaching is in the highest sense teaching, and a marvelous form of teaching at that. I have compared it to teaching a class composed entirely of "A" students, people already committed, eager to learn, and sometimes astonishingly fast learners. Second, I came to appreciate that much more gets taught than technique -- I shall speak more to this presently. Third, through coaching I gained access to a host of issues about knowing and the development of knowledge which were a consequence largely of the physical dimension of the game. I shall take up this rich issue in detail in later chapters.

All of which brings me to the present book, which, as I have tried here to suggest, has been germinating for quite a while. There remain a few preliminary issues to discuss before I move to the body of the book.

I shall not begin with a definition of play. As my discussion in Part II will reveal, I am not convinced that such a definition can be given or even whether, if it could be, it would be needful. But I am convinced that the beginning, contrary to the view of many, is not the place even to consider the project of a definition. The impetus to begin a project such as this by "defining our terms" or "getting clear on our basic concepts" seems based on the model of an axiomatic system in mathematics, and I have already argued that play is of a nature that its reflective clarification cannot be modeled after the procedures of the mathematical sciences. If a "definition" were to emerge at all, it would have to be in the course of and as a result of our reflections, and as the reader shall see, even this enterprise I regard as questionable.

Second, there are some associations which the notion of play calls to mind which I think can be dispensed with at the beginning because they have already been disposed of by the growing literature on play. I refer to the contrasts which we are wont to draw in our unreflective moments between play and work, and play and seriousness, as if play could not involve both hard work and the deepest seriousness. As is no doubt obvious even from my introductory autobiographical remarks, I have always found play altogether compatible with work and with seriousness, and I am inclined to attribute the dichotomies to a "protestant ethic" as misguided as it is unplayful. The play of this book will attempt to exhibit both work and high seriousness.

PART I

Chapter 1: The Sociological Standpoint

As I indicated in the Preface, I intend in Part I to take up and evaluate some of the dominant standpoints from which play has been understood traditionally, attempting to appreciate both their contributions and limitations. As such, my effort in these chapters will be in part a critique in the Kantian sense, an effort to establish what kind of insights each standpoint can discover, and at the same time what the limits of that standpoint are. As I earlier put it in the Heideggerian mode, we need to determine what each standpoint, as the standpoint it is, reveals and conceals. But that is not the only intention of these early chapters. In each case, leading spokesmen for each standpoint have made certain specific claims and contributions which are particularly thought-provoking or controversial, and which need to be considered and reflected upon. Accordingly, each of the succeeding three chapters will have these two projects. As anyone who has engaged in such "transcendental" investigations knows, it is neither possible nor desirable to keep these two enterprises utterly separate, and so I shall not even attempt to avoid their overlap.

It is fair to say that the dominant way in which play, and especially sports, are studied today is from the sociological standpoint. By this I mean that much of the attention -- and some of the best insights -- is focused upon play as a contemporary cultural phenomenon, upon the role of play in society (and I shall be using the term "sociological" in no more technical sense than this). Perhaps not surprisingly, this approach has tended to focus more on the "sports" phenomenon than on the more general and therefore more opaque phenomenon of play. Still, it should suit our purposes, since although sport is evidently not the whole of play, it is just as evidently part of play, and so can be legitimately taken as an example of our subject matter (the question of the exact nature -- and value -- of such distinctions as those between "play", "sport", "athletics", "games", etc. can be taken up in a later chapter).

The most general thesis of the sociological standpoint is that sport or play is to be understood and, for those sociologists who believe in value judgments, evaluated, as a manifestation of certain

1

situations, certain values, certain problems, in the society at large. Typically then, the situation in sport is taken to be a reflection of some influence of society and moreover is taken to be explained by that influence. Thus Jack Scott says in the Preface to his thought-provoking book, The Athletic Revolution,

> "Interscholastic and intercollegiate athletic programs are usually a microcosm of the total educational structure within which they operate."[1]

In his rhetorically more radical Rip Off The Big Game, Paul Hoch asserts,

> "The sports most appreciated in a particular society, and the way in which they are played, in turn reflect the past and present development of that society; they are, in fact, a mirror reflection of that society."[2]

Further,

> "Play is play. It seems to exist in one form or another in all human societies and throughout most of the animal kingdom. But the character of what passes for ´play´ is decisively shaped by the social system in which it occurs; and so too, are both the ´players´ and non-players."[3]

Nor is this position limited to those especially critical of either sport or society. The very chapter titles of a book, Sport and American Society, by George Sage, reveal the same fundamental orientation: Chapter 1: "The Social Study of Sport in American Society"; Chapter 2: "The Heritage of Sport in America"; Chapter 3: "Socialization and Sport"; Chapter 4: "Social Stratification and Sport"; Chapter 5: "Women and Sport"; Chapter 6: "Race and Sport"; Chapter 7: "Social Change and Sport"; and Chapter 8: "Sport and the School". In the same book, in an article entitled "The Interdependence of Sport and Culture", Gunther Luschen states straightforwardly,

2

"Sport is indeed an expression of that sociocultural system in which it occurs."[4]

Now it is important to appreciate the direction of influence here, which moves from society to sport rather than vice-versa. The clear implication of the sociological theses is that values, problems, or attitudes arise first in society at large and then are reflected in the sport or play situation. To be sure, and as we shall presently discuss, sports are often said by supporters and critics alike to teach values. But the sociological point is that the values that get taught derive from society. Thus, to take now standard examples, if sports in America are troubled by racism or sexism, that is because American society is so troubled. Or more positively, if sports are said to teach courage or self-discipline, this shows that society holds these values in high regard.

Now few would want to dispute the correctness of this thesis. The problems of racism and sexism in American sports, to continue with those examples, have been documented beyond dispute, and since there is next to no evidence that sports are <u>inherently</u> racist or sexist, a reasonable supposition is that these troubles are injected into the sport or play situation from society at large. But the thesis does raise some important questions. Taken in its strong form, that play or sport is a reflection -- even a "mirror reflection" -- of society, it implies that play or sport has no intrinsic character of its own, no values, lessons, or attitudes, inherent in play which <u>it</u> might inject into society, thus reversing or at least countering the direction of influence from society to sports. But surely we have to take this question seriously: does sport or play have inherent characteristics not derived from a given society but perhaps more primordial than that society, which might be injected into society itself? If so, we shall have to ask whether those characteristics are desirable or not, and so how their inculcation into society may be encouraged or inhibited. My first point, then, is that there seems to be an asymmetry to the sociological standpoint's thesis regarding sport and society: the direction of influence seems always from society to the play sphere, whereas I am suggesting we ought at least to entertain, within the standpoint of sociology itself (that is, within the problematic of the relation of play and society), the possibility of a reciprocal influence and its consequences.

The issue is made somewhat more complicated by the presence of a second prevalent thesis, one that argues that sports do in fact teach or inculcate lessons, attitudes, and especially values. This thesis is supported both by those who affirm and by those who deplore the values being taught. Writers such as Scott and Hoch certainly hold that sports teach values; they happen to deplore the values that they see being taught -- racism, sexism, authoritarianism, dog-eat-dog competitiveness, the "win at any cost" attitude, and the like. In a passage that borders on self-parody of this sort of criticism, Hoch has occasion to say,

> "We can, then, see how different sports,
> the sports industry, and the ideology of
> sports, arose as a consequence of the
> developing material conditions of capitalist
> society, and how the sports industry
> functioned to facilitate the smoothness of
> authoritarian capitalist class relations
> generally; how it helped socialize workers
> for their coglike roles on the assembly
> lines; how it built up a symbiotic relation-
> ship with the developing mass media industry;
> how sports and the media helped socialize
> workers to think of themselves mainly as
> passive consumers; how sports spread the
> poisons of competitiveness, elitism, sexism,
> nationalism, militarism, and racism -- all
> of which have kept the international working
> class divided against itself; and, finally,
> how there has developed within the sports
> world itself a movement of athletes to build
> a more human society."[5]

On the other hand, we are all familiar with the praise of the educational value of sport such as occurred in a recent article in Time Magazine, a magazine which might well be subtitled "The Journal of Pop-Sociology."

> "Sport has always been one of the primary
> means of civilizing the human animal, of
> inculcating the character traits a society
> desires. Wellington in his famous aphorism
> insisted that the Battle of Waterloo had
> been won on the playing fields of Eton. The
> lessons learned on the playing field are
> among the most basic: the setting of goals

4

and the joining with others to achieve them;
an understanding of and respect for rules;
the persistence to hone ability into skill,
prowess into perfection. In games, children
learn that success is possible and that
failure can be overcome. Championships may
be won; when lost, wait till next year. In
practicing such skills as fielding a grounder
and hitting a tennis ball, young athletes
develop work patterns and attitudes that
carry over into college, the marketplace,
and all of life."[6]

Now this thesis, that play teaches us, is an
extremely old one. It is, for example, virtually
built into the etymology of the Greek words for play
and education, _paidia_ and _paideia_ respectively. If
play is genuinely educational, one might conclude that
that in itself establishes its decisive importance,
and lead one to wonder why for so long the subject has
lacked academic respectability. Still, it must be
noted that implicit in both the positive and negative
versions of this thesis is the claim that play takes
its fundamental reference from outside itself, that it
is to be evaluated, favorably or not, according to
some sphere other than play itself.

As with the first thesis so here, we can accept
the correctness of the view that play inculcates
values and yet ask, is this adequate? If the
essential value of play itself is that it teaches
values, then again play seems to be granted no
inherent nature of its own, as can be seen if we
consider the consequences on this view for those who
decide that the values taught by sports are
predominantly negative. If one holds this view, then
it would seem to follow that one ought to eliminate
sports, a thesis that more than one critic of sport
has maintained. To avoid this inference, one would
have to show, just as I suggested regarding the first
thesis, that play and sport have their own nature,
their own values and attitudes, and so their own
integrity.

Superficially, the thesis that sport teaches us
values might be taken as the reciprocal of the thesis
that society's values are reflected in sport and play,
but as I have already indicated, this is not so. The
first thesis has a clear priority. To be sure, sports

5

teaches values, but those values are themselves a reflection of the society itself, of its desires and its standards. The genuine consequence of putting the two theses together would thus seem to be less a reciprocal relationship between play and social values as that, for better or worse, play, and especially sport, are propaganda vehicles for existing societal values, standards, and conditions. To repeat, this view is implicitly held both by critics of sport and society and by its supporters.

That sport and play reflect the values and standards as well as the problems of society, and that moreover, play teaches those values and standards to participants, together comprise what I have called the sociological standpoint regarding play. As I have already suggested, the correctness of this general standpoint, the ability to gain genuine insight into both sport and society therefrom, has been documented beyond dispute. To be sure, lively, even bitter debate can occur among spokesmen for that standpoint -- especially, as we have seen, over whether the values reflected and inculcated are worth preserving or not. This in no way calls into question the validity of the general standpoint. But I do wish now to raise questions about its limitations, an issue about which, perhaps understandably, its spokesmen rarely speak. All too often works written from this standpoint give the impression that it is the definitive one from which to understand play, that it offers a comprehensive, even complete understanding of the subject. This need not be stated explicitly; the impression can be and often is given simply by failing to acknowledge that its standpoint, however correct, is one-sided, that it offers at best part of the story.

How, then, might the sociological thesis be shown to be incomplete, its limits or horizons revealed? In the light of what has been said so far, at least two ways come to mind. First and most fundamentally, the limits could be drawn by showing that there is some essential aspect to play which is not simply a reflection of or consequence of society. Perhaps there is something about play which can only be understood from the individual psychological standpoint (the subject of the next chapter). Or perhaps there is something about play which is more fundamental than either society or psychology. Perhaps there is a fundamental relationship between

6

play and human being itself which is independent of any particular society or even society generally. If so, and it is my intention in Part II of this book to show that it is so, then certain limits of the sociological standpoint would be established. This would in no sense entail abandoning it; it has far too many demonstrable insights for that. Rather, it would then take its place and so be placed alongside other, perhaps even more fundamental standpoints. The details of the position that play has a significance independent of and prior to its relation to society of course remains to be established at length. Here I am concerned to establish the structural point that if such is the case, the sociological standpoint, which begins with the assumption of the relation of play and society and procedes from that point, could not in principle gain access to such an inherent significance short of abandoning its own foundational thesis. Such, then, would be one limitation to the sociological position.

Second and somewhat derivitive of the first, a limit could be established by showing that there was something about play or sport which constituted not a reflection of but a critique of society, that the play situation again and again, in a variety of societies, generates values and attitudes counter to the prevailing ones, or at least values not prevalent in society itself. This view is somewhat hilariously adumbrated by Michael Novak in his book, The Joy of Sports, where he claims to have discovered that there are values or qualities derivable virtually only from sports (he hedges on this), and therefore that those who do not participate in sport lack such values. He says,

> "I have never met a person who disliked
> sports, or who absented himself or herself
> entirely from them, who did not at the
> same time seem to me deficient in humanity.
> I don't only mean that all work and no play
> makes Jack a dull boy, or Jill a dull ms.
> I mean that a quality of sensitivity, an
> organ of perception, an access to certain
> significant truths appear to be missing.
> Such persons seem to me a danger to
> civilization."[7]

Perhaps more soberly, one could argue that play typically functions, or sometimes functions, or could function, as a kind of cultural gad-fly, whereby established values were called into question. If so, if there were values inherent in play independent of and even antagonistic to those of a given society, that would enable us to raise the decisive philosophic question of the source or origin of value altogether, a question which the sociological standpoint, which takes its orientation from the values present in a given society, again could not in principle answer. For that issue we would have to turn to a philosophical understanding of play and of human being.

These are two of the boundaries, the "transcendental horizon", of the sociological standpoint. There may be more; these two strike me as especially important and worthy of subsequent consideration. I wish now to select a few of the more specific problems and theses that occur within the sociological perspective and reflect on them in greater detail.

Critics of what they like to call the "sports establishment" focus perhaps more on the issue of racism in contemporary American sport than any other. And it is undeniable that organized sport has not covered itself with glory on the issue of race relations. The deplorable history of racial prejudice in organized sport does indeed seem to be a "mirror reflection" of racism in society. From outright exclusion to the use of "quotas", from blatant slander to the use of more subtle inuendo, Blacks have found in their participation in sport the same kinds of obstacles that have beset them in society at large. Nor have the leaders in sport -- coaches, managers, directors of athletics -- distinguished themselves on the whole as advocates for racial equality. Of course, there are those who defend organized sport against this charge, who argue that in fact sport, though hardly unblemished, is considerably ahead of society as a whole in the matter of race relations. A favorite piece of evidence for this position is the claim that sports is a "social ladder", a way "out of the ghetto" for minority youths who might otherwise be condemned by environment and prejudice to a low socio-economic status. In high school, playing sports "keeps kids off the streets". If a high school player excels, he (and recently, she) may get a scholarship to college, thereby opening up the possibility of an education otherwise unaffordable. For the very few who excel at the college level, there is the possibility of a lucrative professional contract which sometimes puts the individual in the category of the very wealthy. Now, on the surface, this certainly seems a plausible claim. Playing sports in high school does keep kids off the streets -- at least part of the time. Everyone who follows organized sports knows of dozens of poor youths, black and white, who go to colleges to which they surely never would have applied had they not been star athletes. And we look with a mixture of admiration and envy on those few athletes from poor backgrounds who become millionaires in professional sports. But the critics of organized sports, such as Scott and Hoch, call into question the significance of this evidence. In a chapter of his book, The Athletic Revolution, entitled "Athletics and Social Mobility", Scott points out that the number of poor youths who attain affluence through sports is a miniscule percentage of the total deprived population, and therefore can hardly be used as evidence of the value of sports as a social ladder.

> "For every Broadway Joe Namath there are
> hundreds of sad, disillusioned men
> standing on the streetcorners and sitting
> in the beer halls of Pennsylvania towns
> such as Scranton, Beaver Falls, and
> Altoona."[8]

Surely both sides have a point. On the one hand, it is clear that the path of sports stardom has offered and continues to offer a way by which poor people can find their way to fame and fortune. This I daresay is an undeniable fact. But it is equally true that the percentage of the total population of poor youths who actually accomplish this achievement is miniscule indeed, and therefore it is somewhat misleading to praise organized sports for its contributions to social mobility. But I believe that behind this issue lies a deeper and sadder social problem alluded to in the above quote from Scott. The problem is not just that few poor youths "make it" in professional sports while many more fail -- a version of "many and called and few are chosen". Rather, the social conditions of many lower socio-economic areas is such that skill in sports gets held up as not just one of, but the best and most visible course out of

9

the ghetto. This is especially true in the urban ghettoes, and is therefore an acute problem for poor urban blacks. The clear evidence is that thousands, perhaps millions of such youths pursue their athletic careers to the detriment of their development in other areas, and especially of their academic preparation. When so many more youths aspire to sports stardom than can possibly succeed, and sacrifice their overall development in order to do so, we get the deplorable phenomenon of all those people who do not quite succeed in organized sport, unprepared for alternative occupations, and so dejected, alienated, unproductive for themselves and for society. As Scott puts the point perhaps too polemically.

> "Gifted black athletes will usually make
> out all right, but what happens to the
> thousands of young unathletic black
> children whose only heroes are sports
> stars? How many brilliant doctors,
> lawyers, teachers, poets, and artists
> have been lost because intelligent but
> uncoordinated black youths have been led
> to believe by a racist society that their
> only chance for getting ahead was to
> develop a thirty foot jump shot or to run
> the hundred in 9.3?"[9]

In short, there lies here a tremendous social problem of false expectations. But we must be careful not to blame sports for the problem. It is not the fault of basketball if it is made to appear more attractive than the study of mathematics or poetry to ghetto youths. The resolution, or perhaps better, the mitigation of this problem would seem to lie not so much in the social devaluation of sports but in the greater evaluation of other pursuits. This is evidently an educational problem, and perhaps even a problem of social priorities for society as a whole. But the fact remains that the issue resides in the sports realm and will be inevitably associated with it.

Perhaps it is best that it does. For it may be that certain lessons can be derived from the play situation itself which can then be applied to our social relations more generally. The example of racism, and more generally prejudice, is a case in point. Consider the common play situation of

10

"choosing up sides" for a game. Since an obvious goal of team selection is to pick the best team so that one´s team will have the best chance of winning, the situation itself, the phenomenon of choosing sides in competitive play, establishes <u>ability</u> as the standard for selection and evaluation of others and oneself. The play situation in this case dictates that people be selected and evaluated according to how good they are. To be sure, criteria brought into the play realm from without -- racism, prejudice of all sorts -- often supercede the "natural" standard of the play situation; but when they do -- and unlike the common situation in society at large -- one pays an immediate and visible price. If, in choosing sides for a sand-lot basketball game, I refuse to choose the kid with the best jump-short because he is black, or I refuse to choose the tall center we need because he is Jewish, I purchase my prejudice at the price of a likely loss in the game and, given the customs of most sand-lot games, sitting down for the rest of the afternoon. Such considerations, which I repeat are dictated by the play situation itself, can be powerful persuaders. They can lead one, unreflectively at first, then with greater awareness, to begin to select one´s teammates according to the standard of ability alone. And as one becomes increasingly conscious of the legitimacy of this standard on the playing field, one can gradually ask, if here, why not more generally, in all my social relations? In short this play situation can offer a powerful lesson in the irrationality of prejudice. Let me add, I know that this is true, because I am being autobiographical in this example; gradual consciousness of my attitudes and values playing basketball, and the desirability of applying those to my life as a whole, was my own first step out of racism, a small step to be sure, but the first decisive step. Long before I was comfortable socializing with blacks at home, I was utterly comfortable socializing with them on the basketball court, where the measure of a man was the accuracy of his jump-shot. It remained for me to wake up, to become conscious of the contradiction between the kinds of standards I applied to human beings in the play situation and those I applied in my other social relations. Clearly, my play values were superior to my social ones.

One might object (and a similar objection is often made against competitive sport) that what I have in fact done is substitute elitism for racism, and

11

that although this might be a slight improvement it is
hardly the telos of human value, nor is elitism a
value not derivable from society. There is certainly
a kernel of truth in this. Competitive sport has
always struck me as containing a natural elitism, but
in a non-pejorative sense of the term. The hackneyed
phrase, "May the best team win" states clearly this
inherent elitism. But it is decisively important that
the elitism we learn in sport is one of ability rather
than social position, economic status, race, or sex.
We learn in this realm the efficacy of selecting
teammates according to ability; if that is elitism, it
should be welcomed with open arms.

The example of racism and the manner in which, in
the sport realm, its defects can become unmistakably
visible, suggests the sense in which values or
standards inherent in play might be seen as superior
to and implicitly critical of certain societal values.
If I have been at all persuasive, then this raises a
set of questions which go far beyond sociology and
which must be pursued as we take up play in its own
terms. What other values are or might be inherent in
play itself? How might they be transferred into our
societal relations? What is their source? Finally,
what is the source of value altogether?

If there is a second area besides racism where
sport has become the locus of controversy today, it is
surely the issue of women's rights, or the problem of
sexism in sport. Again as with racism, the existence
of a pervasive prejudice against women's participation
in athletics has been documented beyond reasonable
dispute. One can practically establish the point by
statistics alone, rehearsing the disparity between the
numbers of male and female participants in sports at
all levels, or the equally large disparity between the
expenditure on sports for women and men at the high
school, college, and professional levels. These are
only the most obvious manifestations of the myriad
more subtle and therefore more insidious ways that
women have been dissuaded from participation in the
very sporting activities which are praised to the
skies for the benefits they confer on young boys. But
it is not these facts that are controversial. What
is, or at least has been, in dispute is whether or not
the situation should be changed, whether women ought
to be encouraged to play as much as men, and therefore
whether they ought to have the same opportunities, and
so financial support, as our male athletes. At stake

12

here, but too often hidden by rhetoric, is the
fundamental philosophical problem of whether or not
men and women differ "by nature", and what the
consequences of these differences or lack thereof are,
or alternatively whether relevant differences are
"societally determined" and therefore, presumably,
available for societal transformation. A fine example
of the ambiguity often inherent in this issue is
present in Michael Novak´s thoughtful if somewhat
polemical encomium to sports, The Joy of Sports.
Novak, a theologian by training, is of course aware of
the philosophical issues just mentioned, and one can
hear them at work in this curiously ambivalent
statement by him of his attitude toward women´s
participation in sports. Speaking of the remarkable
success of the women´s basketball program in the state
of Iowa and its role as a model or challenge for
women´s sports generally, he says,

> "Such a challenge may or may not be worth
> picking up. It is not certain that women
> will -- or ought to -- build up a structure
> of competitive sports. Despite the
> ideology of the moment, it seems plain to
> me that in virtually every known culture,
> athletic competition (as distinct from
> athletic activities) plays a significantly
> lesser role for women than for men. Perhaps
> past traditions can be overturned.
> Perhaps they should be overturned. But
> perhaps they testify to realities more
> important and enduring than present
> ideologies."[10]

Let us try to analyze carefully what is at stake
here. I believe that each side of the debate -- those
who advocate active participation in competitive
sports for women, with the accompanying commitment to
equal opportunity, more equitable expenditure, and the
other reforms exemplified by the now famous Title IX
Legislation, versus those who oppose such equality of
opportunity -- each side has at least two
philosophical positions on which to base their
arguments. The dominant position for those who
advocate more or less the status quo, that is, the
continuation of the practice of encouraging male
athletic competition while maintaining a "benign
neglect" of female participation, rests on an appeal
to differences in nature between men and women. Here,

13

almost immediately, the issue gets complex. No one denies that there are some differences between men and women (our plumbing, for example, and the other obvious physiological differences); the issue is whether the differences make a difference when it comes to deciding on the appropriateness of athletic competition for women. The proponents of the status quo argue that differences between men and women are such that not only should women not compete with men but that athletic competition per se is somehow less congenial to female nature, either because of physiological characteristics or even because of spiritual characteristics of femininity. As a Connecticut judge, ruling against a young woman's efforts to participate on a men's cross-country team, put it succinctly, "Athletic competition builds character in our boys. We do not need that kind of character in our girls."[11] The problem here is that although the physiological differences are empirical matters determinable at least in principle by careful scientific research, the "spiritual" consequences of the physiological differences are much more opaque and more often decided on political than exclusively empirical grounds. This situation is made all the more complex by our recognition that at least some "spiritual" (or social, or behavioral, or cultural) differences are informed by the traditions of social convention. If women have not (until recently) participated as actively as men in competitive sports, is this because they have been inhibited from doing so by nature or by social convention? This ambiguity is the basis of the arguments most often put forward by the proponents of greater participation by women. The relative lack of athletic participation by women in the past, they argue, has next to no physiological or "natural" basis. It is founded almost entirely in social convention, in a societal tradition which has insisted that "a woman's place is in the home" and has established such personality traits as passivity, gentleness, and delicateness as the norms for women. As such, they can -- and ought -- to be overthrown by the present society. Deciding whether an empirical fact (that women have not participated as actively in athletics as men) is founded in nature or social convention is by no means easy. Nor is the problem of deciding, in either case, whether what is the case ought to be the case. But such decisions are precisely what is implied in either of the positions noted so far.

14

Logically, there are at least two other arguments available on this issue, one for each side, although in fact they are not employed as often as the two dominant arguments already presented. One could argue in defense of the status quo that, yes, the attitudes and situations that have inhibited women from active athletic participation are determined socio-economically, they are not a matter of nature, but that furthermore, the socio-economic conditions which originally occasioned the separation and made it valid remain operative today. On grounds of societal economy and a smoothly functioning culture, then, women ought to be kept pretty much out of athletic competition.

Conversely, one might argue in defense of an increasingly active role for women in athletics that this could be justified by nature, that precisely by granting various physiological and even psychological differences between men and women by nature, it remains the case that active competition in play is appropriate and even nature-enhancing for women.

So far, I have simply set out what I regard as the basic conceptual logic of each position regarding the issue and justification of women's participation in competitive sports. I have purposefully avoided a detailed evaluation of either position or even a setting out of the many variations on these basic positions. I do so partly because I wished to bring out the way in which these are the fundamental positions. But I do so as well because I believe that each position has fundamentally misconstrued the very issue of the relation between masculine and feminine nature as it relates to human nature altogether. The detailed presentation and defense of what I regard as the more adequate conception of the relationship will have to await the development of my argument in Parts II and III. Here, I wish only to present its outline, so that its structure may be compared to that of the preceeding positions. Those positions take the question of male/female nature as of foundational importance. Either there are or are not fundamental differences in nature between men and women, and these differences either do or do not imply the appropriateness of athletic participation for women. In my view, however, these issues cannot be adequately resolved until it is recognized that the very question of the difference between male and female nature is not the primordial one. There are indeed differences,

15

but the differences are founded in a more fundamental unity, that of human being itself (as it happens, our nature as erotic). Since the differences are less fundamental, they are in every case subordinate to the deeper unity. Therefore, in reflecting on any question of human being, and specifically here on the question of the appropriateness of athletic competition for women, it must always be kept in mind whether the issue is one which is within the domain of the differences between men and women, or whether it is within the domain of the unity of human being itself. If the former, then the differences will make a difference, and different standards, activities, modes of behavior, may be appropriate. For example, suppose the bone and muscle structure of women and men is sufficiently different (as apparently it is) so that men will typically be physically stronger and bigger than women. This would be a reasonable argument for segregating men and women in those sports where strength and size are particularly relevant, such as tackle football. But if the latter, if, that is, the locus of the issue is discovered to be more fundamentally in some aspect of being human, then the differences will make no difference. Again to take an example, suppose the issue is the propensity of play to be fun. Unless one wanted to argue the dubious thesis that having fun were a property appropriate to one sex only, one would conclude that this is a dimension or quality of human being, and whatever is concluded would hold for all human beings regardless of sex.

I have purposely chosen rather simple and, I hope, obvious examples in order to make clear the structure of my alternative position. Certainly there are more difficult issues, and the difficulty will often hinge on the difficulty of determining whether a given issue, say, competitiveness or aggressiveness, is an issue for human being altogether or for one sex or another. Here I wish only to establish what I regard as the proper ontological framework within which these issues should be considered. As I have indicated, I shall develop and defend that framework in much greater detail in Parts II and III. But before doing so, I wish to consider two other standpoints from which play is often understood, what I have called the psychological and the historical standpoints respectively.

Footnotes, Chapter 1

1). Scott, Jack, The Athletic Revolution, New York, The Free Press, 1971, page VI.
2). Hoch, Paul, Rip Off The Big Game: The Exploitation of Sports by the Power Elite, New York, Anchor Books, 1972, page 7.
3). Ibid, page 29.
4). Sage, George (Editor), Sport and American Society, Second Edition, Reading, Mass., Addison-Wesley, 1974, page 49.
5). Hoch, Paul, op. cit. page 12.
6). Time Magazine, June 26, 1978, page 55.
7). Novak, Michael, The Joy of Sports, New York, Basic Books, 1976, page 44.
8). Scott, Jack, op. cit. page 179.
9). Ibid, page 180-181.
10). Novak, Michael, op. cit. page 335.
11). Sports Illustrated, May 28, 1973, page 95.

Chapter 2: The Psychological Standpoint

The sociological standpoint focused its investigations and understanding of play on the relationship between play in its various modes and society. In doing so, certain genuine insights into play became available. But at the same time, since that standpoint was not comprehensive or total, a critique became appropriate in which some of the limits or boundaries of that standpoint were observed. The situation is similar with the psychological standpoint. This perspective has a variety of manifestations, some of the most important of which we shall take up in turn. These share, however, a fundamental focus on the meaning or significance of play for the individual. Again, there is obviously nothing wrong with this perspective: a criticism of it as a standpoint would be far less productive than an appreciation of its insights. But a critique is not a criticism, and so part of our appreciation of this standpoint must include an awareness of some of the limits or boundaries which circumscribe it in the midst of making possible its important insights.

There are at least three variations on this standpoint whose spokesmen have made important contributions to the literature on play. I shall call these, loosely, the phenomenological, the Zen, and the clinical approaches. In many ways, the philosophical position I shall set out as my own in Part II will share this focus on the individual, and indeed, at least the phenomenological and Zen approaches are often associated as much with philosophy as with psychology. Of this two things may be said briefly. First, I hope in Part II that the differences between my stance and those I shall discuss in this chapter will emerge. Second, in any case, the separation of psychology and philosophy into two different disciplines is of relatively recent origin (precipitated largely by the more exclusive commitment of psychology to the empirical techniques of the natural sciences) and still held suspect by many psychologists and philosophers alike.

I begin with the phenomenological approach. Phenomenology originated as a formal movement with the work of Edmund Husserl in the early part of this century. However, it has come to be understood far more broadly than its founder intended. Whereas

19

Husserl intended phenomenology as a rigorous and strict scientific methodology, it has come to be associated with a much broader movement in Europe and more recently in the United States which focuses on a description of the human experience of the world, its structures and categories, rather than on a projected world "in itself". The application of this movement to the issue of play has not been very pervasive; although a "phenomenology of play" might be a productive investigation, relatively little explicit work has been done in this area.[1] But the phenomenological movement has focused on certain issues which have a direct relation to play, and foremost among these are the phenomenological investigations into what is often called "the lived body". The basic thesis of most phenomenologists who pursue this issue is that the dualism of soul/body, mind/body, or sometimes self/body, which is now standard in western thought through both the philosophic and religious traditions, is an intellectual abstraction which is simply not the way we experience ourselves. Notwithstanding the ubiquitousness of these dichotomies, now virtually built into everyday language, these phenomenologists argue that the way we actually experience ourselves -- what they often call "the lived body" -- involves no such dualism but a unity, not, to be sure, a static unity but a flowing one, a continuum of experiences, some more "bodily", some more "mental" than others, but with no clear dichotomies and certainly no dualism of different "substances", a body and a soul or mind. Calvin O. Schrag, in an article entitled "The Lived Body As A Phenomenological Datum", puts the general point succinctly:

"The phenomenon in question in my body as concretely lived. The body as immediately apprehended is not a corporeal substance which is in some way attached to, or united with, another substance, variously called in the tradition a "soul", "mind", or "self". The body thus conceptualized is a later abstraction and objectivation, which is phenomenologically eviscerated and epistemologically problematic. I experience my body first as a complex of life-movements which are indistinguishable from my experiences of selfness. My primordial experience is one of engagement in a world of concrete projects -- projects which

20

receive their significance through my body as the locus of concern. The distinctions between soul and body, or mind and body, as they have been formulated in the tradition (particularly by Descartes) are reified and objectivized distinctions, foreign to man's experience as it is immediately lived."[2]

We see clearly here the standard phenomenological emphasis on the way humans <u>experience</u> the world -- in this case the way we experience ourselves -- as both the fundamental subject matter and the standard by which an account of things should be judged. In this it stands against those accounts, scientific, religious, and philosophical, which take a different subject matter than the one we experience as fundamental (hydrogen and oxygen molecules rather than water, or "sense data" rather than trees and chairs) and apply different standards of evaluation (mathematical consistency, a priori reasoning, or appeal to religious dogma).

But what has this to do with the phenomenon of play? Perhaps it is obvious. Play, especially those playful activities which involve both "physical" and "mental" dimensions (probably the majority of playful activities), would seem to be decisive evidence for the phenomenological point. In our play we experience precisely that unity of our mental and physical power of activity (N.B. Note how easily the language of dichotomy could be inferred here.) which phenomenologists argue is our primordial experience of ourselves. In play, we experience ourselves as one, we <u>are</u> this immersion-in-activity, be it jogging, skiing, or a championship basketball game. Occasionally, the immersive character of the play experience is so intensified that we get the phenomenon of "peak experiences", about which more will be said presently. Here, the point to understand is that play seems to exhibit in the highest degree a certain conception of human being as a unity or "lived body". Perhaps the point should be made more forcefully. One could say that play is not just one example of this; it is paradigmatic, and insofar as this experience of the unity of mental and physical activity is a <u>desideratum</u>, play becomes something to be recommended as an experience of great value, offering in the highest or deepest sense the primordial, perhaps the truest, experience of

21

ourselves.

Nor is the lived body the only dimension of play where phenomenologists have found a rich field for their investigations. Phenomenological investigations of time, space, equipment, relationality, even pain, have all found clear applicability in the field of play. While phenomenology has found here a fruitful subject matter and confirmation of its own fruitfulness as a philosophical method, the study of play itself has been enriched by the wealth of insights shed by various phenomenologically oriented investigations.

Earlier I alluded to a phenomenon occasionally accessible in play, that of a sense of total immersion in the activity, an experience which in its most intense moments is often described, using Mazlow's terminology, as a "peak experience". The presence and relatively frequent availability of this experience in play has led to the popular application of a second psychologically oriented approach to the study of play, which I have chosen to call, loosely, the Zen approach. Probably the first and still one of the best of such works is Eugen Herrigel's Zen In The Art Of Archery, but its spirit has been followed by such works as George Leonard's The Ultimate Athlete and the plethora of Zen _____ (fill in the blank with your favorite sport) books, Zen Running, Zen Tennis, etc. Basically, the point of this position is that the attitudes, techniques, and philosophies associated with eastern Zen philosophy can be fruitfully applied to various sport activities, usually with better results in the sport, but in any case with a deeper or more meaningful experience for the individual.

The latter contrast points to a very different emphasis in the eastern Zen writings and the way this perspective has been transformed in the western "Zen Sport" books alluded to above. For eastern Zen, the role of archery, or martial arts, or flower arranging, is as a means to a different and presumably more important end than excellence at the activity, although it happens that Zen Masters typically are astonishingly adept at the activity. The real end is the state of heightened awareness, enlightenment, or Nirvana to which practice of the Zen activity may lead. In its western applications, however, the central point of practicing the Zen approach seems to be to improve your game. In an analogous way, some of

22

the fruits of the clinical psychological approach to be discussed presently get used not as they were originally intended, for the benefit of the individual in question, but for the benefit of coaches, who can use psychological insight to "get more out of" their players.

Teachings central to the Zen position usually include a long period of training, typically under a "master" (Herrigel, for example, studied archery under a master for six years), a beginning period of great concentration and intellectual effort which gradually gives way to a sense of effortless "letting go", of not having to "think" about what one is doing, almost of purposelessness, or as Herrigel puts it, of "artless art", and finally, commensurate with the latter, a gradual "forgetting of self", "letting go of the will", which in its extreme form becomes a kind of self-less immersion typically associated with mystical experience. Thus in the introduction to Herrigel's book, D.T. Suzuki writes,

> "If one really wishes to be master of an art, technical knowledge of it is not enough. One has to transcend technique so that the art becomes an "artless art" growing out of the Unconscious. In the case of archery, the hitter and the hit are no longer two opposing objects, but are one reality. The archer ceases to be conscious of himself as the one who is engaged in hitting the bull's-eye which confronts him. This state of unconsciousness is realized only when, completely empty and rid of the self, he becomes one with the perfecting of his technical skill, though there is in it something of a quite different order which cannot be attained by any progressive study of the art."[3]

Moreover, the master, in response to one of Herrigel's queries on how to achieve his goal, replies,

> "By letting go of yourself, leaving yourself and everything yours behind you so decisively that nothing more is left of you but a purposeless tension."[4]

23

George Leonard, speaking directly of the applicability
of all this to athletics, says in The Ultimate
Athlete,

> "Having no tradition of mystical experience,
> no adequate mode of discourse on the
> subject, no preparatory rites, the athlete
> might refuse to enter (the door to "infinite
> realms of perception and being"). But the
> athletic experience is a powerful one, and
> it may thrust the athlete, in spite of fear
> and resistance, past the point of no return,
> into a place of awe and terror."[5]

Probably one of the great contributions of this
so-called eastern way of thinking on the play
experience is that it has made respectable, by
founding it in a venerable intellectual tradition,
discussion about certain kinds of very profound,
moving experiences available in athletics which most
western athletes, through their own peculiar
tradition, had almost in embarrassment kept to
themselves: the peak experience. But there are also
issues of great philosophic interest therein. Here I
shall mention only a few. I shall only raise them as
issues at this point, since their deeper development
and adequate understanding will be accomplished
subsequent to the development of my own understanding
of play.

The first issue arises out of the teaching,
common in eastern thought generally and clearly
present in books such as Zen In The Art Of Archery and
The Ultimate Athlete, that one decisive aspect of
enlightenment, or of the totally immersive experience
available in play, is the experience of the loss or
even destruction of the self. I have already cited
passages which refer explicitly to the desirability of
achieving "selflessness". But several questions arise
here. First and perhaps most basically, what does,
what could, this mean? More specifically, what is the
conception of self at work here such that one could
"lose" the self yet still be, still experience that
loss? To say the least, the conception of the self
operative needs to be worked out and understood.
Second, supposing that we do agree on a conception of
the self such that it is possible to "lose" it, is
this loss desirable, and if so, why? For people who
happen to like themselves, is the loss of the self not

24

an altogether undesirable possibility to be studiously avoided? Third, if one is going to speak in such metaphors as losing the self (is it a metaphor?), could not one suggest that, to the contrary, it is precisely in play, and especially in the most intense play experiences, that we <u>find</u> ourselves, that we become who we can be? According to the famous remark of Schiller, "Man plays only when he is in the full sense of the word a man, and he is only wholly Man when he is playing."[6] If anything like that is so, then truly in play we do not lose but find our selves. To repeat, then, these questions, all genuine questions and not rhetorical, are clearly founded in the first; and the working out of a conception of what the self is is so closely tied to the nature of play itself that it must await an adequate presentation in Part II. But the questions must be preserved.

The next general issue centers on the nature and possibility of the "mystical" experience and its relation to play. Related to this is the question of the now well-documented occurrence of "peak experiences" in play. Are such "peak experiences" essentially the same as the eastern "mystical" experience? If not, what are the differences? Compare, for example, the description of the mystical experience taken from Herrigel and cited above, with the following remarks on peak experiences among athletes taken from an unpublished article by Kenneth Ravizza entitled "A Study of the Peak Experience in Sport":

> "Frequently during the peak experience, each of the athletes recalled, he was so involved in the experience that he lost sight of his "normal" conscious self. Some athletes went further -- their involvement caused them to become one with the experience. A woman discus thrower explained, ´I became motion, for all purposes I was motion´".[7]

At first glance, the two experiences seem very similar if not identical. Yet immediately one problem arises which can perhaps best be presented by an anecdote from one of my courses on the philosophy of sport. In that course, which had an enrollment of about 40 undergraduates, I began our discussion of Herrigel´s <u>Zen In The Art Of Archery</u> by offering a few

25

citations regarding the mystical experience, including those quoted above, and then asked how many of the students felt that they had had a mystical experience. Not a single student replied affirmatively. Later, in a class devoted to an examination of the peak experience, I went through a similar procedure, first describing the experience, quoting the above, and then asking how many of the students felt that they had had a peak experience in play. In this case, however, all but a handful of the students responded affirmatively! What was at work here? My guess is as follows: especially in our culture, discussions of mystical experiences are usually presented with an aura about them of near inaccessibility or at least of privileged access, of once in a lifetime uniqueness, which leads one to believe that even one's most intense, most meaningful experiences could not compare, of course, with the dramatic descriptions of the mystical experience. Herrigel himself contributes to this. For example, he presents the information that he studied archery for six years, practicing almost daily at his exercises, in such a way as to give the impression of an extraordinary feat of commitment, something almost none of us ever do. Yet when, in less dramatic language, I asked my students (many of whom were intercollegiate athletes) whether any of them had _not_ worked very hard, practicing almost daily at their chosen sport for at least six years, it became clear at once that this experience, far from being reserved for those unique few with a Herculean (or Herrigelian) capacity for commitment, was available to almost all of them. The question then is, is the kind of experience which "Zen sport" writers describe a unique experience for the privileged few, as the language of the mystical experience often suggests? Or is it, without losing any of its extraordinary meaningfulness and profundity, available to us all, and in fact have not most of us already had it if we only reflect on it and describe it in the slightly more moderate language of peak experiences? If so, if play, that is, offers us an occasion in _its_ nature where this kind of exhilarating experience is readily available, and if it is desirable, then this alone would suggest a great psychological significance to the phenomenon of play.

The third position associated with the psychological standpoint I have called the clinical. The best exemplar of this approach is Arnold Beisser's fine book, The Madness In Sport.[8] In perhaps the most

26

conspicuously psychological spirit of the three positions here discussed, Beisser, a psychiatrist, applies his psycho-analytic techniques to athletes who have come to him for help. Beisser presents a series of case studies, then several more general chapters. In so doing, he shows that reflection on one's involvement in play can be a rich source of psychological insight into oneself, presumably as rich for those of us who consider ourselves psychologically "healthy" as for those of us with more obvious psychological troubles. Let me detail some of the kinds of insights Beisser's analysis reveals.

In talking to his patients, Beisser is particularly sensitive to the significance of the kind of sports one plays, and to the mode of involvement in it. Since the organization of his book is fundamentally in terms of case studies, he has not ordered his examples in any systematic way. Let me try to do so, adding a few of my own. Regarding the choice of sports, the following aspects of one's choice might be psychologically revealing:

a). Sociological status: Suppose your three favorite sports are polo, equestrian events, and squash; obviously you are inclined toward "aristocratic" sports, associated with wealth and upper class life. Are you indeed from that class? If so, are you satisfied with letting your choice of sports be so overtly influenced by your class background? What does this tell you about yourself? If you are not from the upper class, the question arises as to the extent to which you are using sports as a "social ladder". Are you satisfied with this? (One of Beisser's case studies concerned just such a situation). Conversely, suppose your favorite sports are basketball, boxing, and Double Dutch: depending on whether you are from an upper or lower socio-economic class, what does this preference tell you about yourself?

b). Competitive vs. non-competitive sports: do you enjoy sports such as jogging, and cross-country skiing, but avoid overtly competitive sports? Or vice-versa? Are you "taking out your aggressions" in competitive sports, or revealing your pathological fear of expressing your own aggressive feelings by avoiding such sports? If so, again, what does this suggest about yourself? Are you satisfied with your preference, or are you missing something important?

Or fleeing from something important?

c). Team vs. individual sports: suppose your
favorite sports are tennis, golf and wrestling, or
conversely, basketball, football, and soccer. What
does this suggest about your conception of your self
and the nature of your relations with others? If you
tend to individual sports, does this show solid
independence or a fear of close relationships and
cooperation? If you tend to team sports, does this
suggest a healthy sense of relationality or a
troublesome dependence on others? If you enjoy both
kinds, does this show well-roundedness or an
indecisiveness regarding your attitudes towards
others? The specifics will of course differ for
different individuals. The question is, what does
one's choice suggest about oneself?

d). Contact vs. non-contact sports: a number
of potentially revealing issues are present here. If
one likes sports involving physical contact, is it
excessive aggression or a healthy exhuberance
regarding one's own and others' bodies? Conversely
does the avoidance of contact suggest a healthy lack
of aggression or a pathological <u>malaise</u> about the
body? In this regard, it is worth noting that
generally, physical contact, both of the aggressive
sort and the more gentle forms such as hugging,
patting, and kissing, is far more acceptable in the
sport realm than it is in society at large. Teammates
pat each other, hug, kiss, cry at victory and defeat,
and in general display emotions that in most
situations they have been trained to suppress. It is
both interesting and puzzling that this freedom, this
reduction of inhibition, has been granted to the play
world. Whether the explanation is sociological,
psychological, or built into the freedom and
exhuberance of play itself is a difficult question.
Here its presence need only be noted as an element in
the general issue of the significance of physical
contact in play.

e). Co-educational vs. non-co-educational
sports: this is an increasingly pervasive issue as
women take a more active role in sports. As the issue
is sometimes put, it seems that women's bodies, which
have for so long been "protected" from physically
active sports, turn out to be not nearly so fragile as
are male egos. Do those men who are reluctant to play
against women do so out of fear of being "humiliated"

if they should lose? Why should losing in a game be humiliating at all? Why more so if a man loses to a woman? Why should the play situation be a place where one's sexuality is placed in question? If you are a woman, do you get a special pleasure out of beating men? Or do you find yourself not quite playing your best against men you suspect you can beat? Once again, a sensitivity to some of the nuances of this dimension can raise revealing, and troublesome, problems for us all.

f). Spectator vs. non-spectator sports: if most of the sports that you play involve having large numbers of people watch you, to what extent are you "in it for the glory"? A show-off? Desperate for recognition? Or is all this quite healthy? Again, does an avoidance of spectator sports on your part suggest a healthy indifference to fickle fame or a pathological lack of confidence?

g). Sports emphasizing physical strength and dexterity vs. those emphasizing more finesse and intelligence: an interesting variant on this is the distinction drawn in various sports between "skill positions" (e.g. quarterback in football, catcher and pitcher in baseball) and other, presumably "non-skill" positions. Again, one's choice of sport or position can be revealing concerning one's self-image, aspirations, or fears.

There are no doubt other possible categories. But I hope enough has been said to bring home the general point. The choices of sports or play opportunities which we usually make unreflectively can, if reflected upon, be psychologically informative about ourselves and can raise a set of issues about the psychological significance of these choices that are thought-provoking in themselves. The same is true for the mode of involvement that we have in our chosen sport. Here, we see such problems as these: people who "can't win", who typically "fold in the clutch" (Beisser usually interprets this as revelatory of unconscious guilt feelings); poor losers; people who only play well, or at least play better, when alienated from their opponent; "selfish" players who, although they choose to play team sports, cannot be good "team players"; poeple who strive at sports at which they are at a physical disadvantage (My own case is amusing here. Why in the world, as a person of 5'8", did I commit myself to playing basketball, where my small stature was an ever-present disadvantage to be overcome?); or finally, the phenomenon of the "injury prone" athlete. Is this merely physical or are there other factors involved?

Again, the point is not to make the list exhaustive but to bring home the recognition that careful reflection on our choice of sports and mode of involvement in them can be a source of genuine self-knowledge, especially on the psychological level.

We can now turn to the limits or horizon of the psychological standpoint as we have examined it. No doubt there are certain limitations peculiar to each of the three specific approaches I considered. Here I am interested in the "transcendental horizon" of the psychological standpoint in general.

The psychological standpoint focuses on the meaning and significance of play for the individual, in contrast to the sociological standpoint which concentrates its attention at the level of society. As they so often do, therefore, the psychological and sociological standpoints have -- or ought to have -- a relationship of reciprocity. Both need each other to fill out their respective accounts. Because they focus on different levels of experience their positions, though indeed different, are not at all incompatible. If there is an "argument" between them, it would be on the issue of priority, and so one will sometimes hear spokesmen for the psychological standpoint arguing that their standpoint, and so their insights, are prior and more fundamental than those of sociology, a position itself founded on the complex and controversial issue of the relationship and priority of the individual and society. Still, it remains the case that the presence of each position does reveal an important limit on the other. In the present case, the psychological standpoint, in focusing its attention on the individual, only focuses on the individual, and so needs the sociological standpoint as a step toward a more comprehensive understanding of the human situation regarding play.

The second decisive limitation is one shared with most versions of the sociological standpoint. I refer to the attempt to "avoid value judgments" in one's investigations, to keep one's research "value free". Of this propensity we need note two things. First, it is often associated with the effort of a position to become "scientific", which entails imitating as much as possible the methodological principles of the natural sciences, which in turn, since the 17th century rise of modern science, have included the avoidance of value judgments. That is no doubt one root of the non-normative standpoint of the phenomenological and clinical approaches. But it is not a comprehensive explanation, as is obvious from the very presence of what I earlier called the Zen approach. This approach certainly does not claim to be scientific in the modern sense, yet it shares with the other positions the avoidance of value judgments. To take only one acute example to which I have already alluded, the Zen approach recommends an experience in which "the self" is annihilated. To say the least, some of us would want a sustained argument as to why it is good to destroy the self, and by inference, why the self is bad and needs to be annihilated. Yet such discussions, which amount to a "value-full" account of the self, are as difficult to find in the Zen approach as in the other psychological and sociological approaches.[9] Consequently, although the limitation of science is certainly one source of the avoidance of value questions in the psychological standpoint, it is not the only one. Second, it is important to appreciate that this avoidance of questions of value is often self-conscious and intentional, done, in the case of the scientific orientation, in order to "be scientific". The fact remains, however, that if these approaches, all of them, avoid value judgments, yet if the subject matter of their investigation is one in which value is inherent, then the approach will perforce be limited and decisively incomplete. This is precisely the case, I shall argue, with play. It may be that one can examine hydrogen and oxygen molecules, make no value judgments, yet adequately comprehend them. But there may be subjects, such as play, in which the value-question, whether and in what circumstances the activity is good or bad, healthy or unhealthy, noble or disgraceful, is so fundamental that no adequate account could be given which did not take a stand on these questions. Those positions, therefore, which on principle avoided such questions would be decisively limited in regard to such subjects. Thus we can well accept the valuable insights of the approaches discussed so far without being satisfied that they are comprehensive. We must seek for an approach -- or approaches -- which go beyond their limitations.

31

Footnotes, Chapter 2

1). Some noteworthy exceptions can be found, for example, in Sport and the Body: A Philosophical Symposium, edited by Ellen Gerber and William Morgan, Second Edition, Philadelphia, Lea and Febiger, 1979.

2). Gerber and Morgan (eds.) op. cit. page 143.

3). Herrigel, Eugen, Zen In The Art Of Archery, New York, Vintage Books, 1971, page 10.

4). Ibid, page 52.

5). Leonard, George, The Ultimate Athlete, New York, Viking Press, 1974, page 40.

6). Schiller, Friedrich, On The Aesthetic Education of Man, In A Series of Letters, translated by Reginald Snell, New York, Frederick Ungar Publishing Co., 1965, page 80.

7). Ravizza, Kenneth, "A Study of the Peak Experience in Sport", unpublished paper, pages 5-6.

8). Beisser, Arnold, The Madness In Sport, Second Edition, Bowie, Md., The Charles Press Publishers, 1977.

9). Marxist and quasi-Marxist positions such as those of Scott and Hoch, are clear exceptions.

Chapter 3: The Historical Standpoint

The historical standpoint, as the name implies, studies and understands play from the perspective of its historical development. Its most general thesis is clear enough; play, like so many human things, is a cultural phenomenon, and as such develops historically. Moreover, to know a phenomenon one must know its origins, and to know origins it is imperative to study the history of the phenomenon in question, whether it be a country, an evolved species, or a phenomenon such as play. To understand play, therefore, one needs to study that historical development. This means studying a variety of cultures to see how play shows itself in each, and how the concept develops through the development of the cultures. One might attempt to understand play in a single culture, e.g. "play in Comanche culture", or one might proceed comparatively, comparing, say, oriental with western concepts of play, or one might aim for comprehensiveness, studying play as it develops in all cultures, or at least in a sufficiently large number to be able to risk some inductive generalizations. In any of these cases, the founding assumption remains the same, that, again, to understand play in one or many or all cultures, the proper procedure is to trace the historical development of the concept.

It is easy to see that this procedure can be a source of rich insight. Some of the most valuable historical insights have centered on the origins of sports within various other cultural phenomena. For example, it is now common knowledge that the ancient Greek Olympics were intimately tied to religious celebration. We know also that the same close connection between sport and religious experience is present in a number of other cultures, from North American Indian tribes to the Incas, from rituals in African tribes to the now famous instances of Zen sports discussed in the previous chapter. To be sure, we in western culture now no longer tie our sporting activity explicitly to orthodox religion (although such groups as the Fellowship of Christian Athletes give one pause). But might there not be an echo of this early connection in the ritualistic character of so much of our sporting activity, in the sense of "sacred space" and "sacred time" often granted to sport contests, and in the intimate and sometimes

33

passionate involvement of the spectators in the game itself? At least one well-known writer on the topic has insisted at length on this connection. Novak, in his previously cited The Joy of Sports, makes a powerful case for the religious roots of many aspects of contemporary sports.

A second important connection that historical studies have revealed is that between sport and various socio-economic classes. It seems, for example, that most sports which involve getting a ball past an opponent's goal (soccer, football, rugby) derive from medieval peasant games involving the pushing of a large boulder from one castle to another. Racquet sports, on the other hand, have their origin in the much more genteel pastimes of the aristocracy. Moreover, the number of sports whose origins can be traced to war activities is manifold, from track events such as racing or javelin throwing, to boxing, to the various equestrian events associated with the "captains" of war. Do not these insights continue to shed light on the socio-economic status of various contemporary sports, a factor which, as a previous discussion has indicated, can play such an important role in our choices of sports?

The last example mentioned, the original connection between various sports and war-related activities, raises the very important and controversial issue of the connection between war and play. General Douglas McArthur's famous remark to the effect that "On the friendly fields of strife are sown the seeds which, on other fields, will bear the fruits of victory", testifies to the positive connection some have found between war and sports. The aphorism, "Sports make men" usually alludes to the development of such war-related virtues as courage, aggressiveness, and discipline. But others have criticized sports for precisely this connection, arguing that the playing of sports conceived in imitation of war activities will simply perpetuate the warlike mentality that we want so much to diminish. Still others, and I shall subsequently take my stand with this group, argue that it is a misconstrual of the true nature of play to relate it closely to war. Whatever one's position on this issue, the evidence which historical studies of sports present concerning their original connections to war activities is important and necessary to interpret.

34

Without doubt, the outstanding spokesman for this standpoint in the study of play is Johan Huizinga, whose book, Homo Ludens, is a classic not just in the historical study of play but in the literature of play altogether. Because of its stature, its dominance, and its seminal character as a paradigm of the historical standpoint, I shall focus my remarks regarding this position on this important book.

Huizinga studies the history of the play concept, or what he calls the "play element", in a variety of cultures. As his chapter headings suggest, he focuses on the role of play in a number of important cultural phenomena; thus in "Play and Law" we see how play functions within the legal frameworks of several ancient cultures. The case is similar with chapter topics such as "Play and War", "Play and Knowing", "Play and Poetry", "Play-Forms in Philosophy", and "Play-Forms in Art". Sometimes surprisingly, Huizinga finds play lurking under seemingly every important cultural phenomenon, in every culture that he studies. Perhaps this is what leads him to the strong opening statement of his thesis, not simply that play is worth studying in its own right, not simply that play is an element which sheds light on culture, but that "For many years the conviction has grown upon me that civilization arises and unfolds in and as play."[1] Clearly, then, and this is one of the great appeals of the book, Huizinga takes play with great seriousness. He is as far as possible from the common -- and condescending -- view that play is of minor significance, on the periphery of human life and culture. On the contrary, in what risks the converse overstatement, Huizinga argues that play is utterly central to the development of culture. His examples from the various cultural phenomena alluded to in the table of contents, then, are directed to showing not merely the presence of play throughout the histories of cultures but its centrality to those cultures. He does so at considerable length and with thorough scholarship.

As with anyone who takes an historical approach to the examination of a given issue, Huizinga faces an initial problem of considerable importance. He wishes to examine play historically. Should he begin with his own conception of play, or the conception of play generally accepted within his own culture? If so, he risks imposing a contemporary and possibly provincial conception of play on other cultures and even on

earlier epochs in his own culture to which it is
foreign, and so bound to be misleading. At first and
in a decisive respect, Huizinga seems to fall into
precisely this problem. On page three of his text, he
characterizes play as "resist(ing) all analysis, all
logical interpretation"[2]; he adds that it is "this
fun-element that characterizes the essence of play"[3],
adds further that play "cannot have its foundations in
any rational nexus"[4], and so concludes a page later
that "play is irrational"[5]. Now the problem here is
obvious; if Huizinga abides by this initial
understanding of play, he will accept as play in other
cultures only those activities and attitudes which
conform to this conception. His will be an
"essentialist" theory, arguing that there is an
"essence" to play, and only insofar as a given
activity conforms to that essence will it genuinely be
play. But what if there are cultures which do not
agree with this conception, which might even
contradict it by holding to a conception of play as
paradigmatically rational and intelligible? Evidently
the imposition of Huizinga's own understanding would
risk distorting our comprehension of other cultures'
understanding of play.

But notwithstanding Huizinga's initial
characterizing of what he calls "the essence of
play"[6], he makes no such distortion but rather
follows a distinctly different procedure. Huizinga's
real method is to look at the various cultures being
studied to see how they use the term play, what
activities and attitudes they regard as play. He is
especially sensitive to the etymologies of words for
play in various languages, and of the etymological
connections between the words for play and words
central to various cultural phenomena such as law,
war, art, and philosophy. He is thus able to find
"the play element" in these phenomena. To take a now
well-known example, Huizinga cites the etymological
significance of the Greek word agon (contest) and
easily relates it to the war situation, thereby tying
together play and war.[7] Again, he sees the
etymological kinship between the Greek words for
"play" and "education" (paidia and paideia
respectively) and so is able to make that important
connection.[8] In short, Huizinga's real method is to
follow in effect the Wittgensteinian principle, "Don't
look for the meaning, look for the use." He sees how
each culture in question uses the concept of play, and
if a given culture calls a given activity play, it is

play -- at least for that culture.

In so doing, Huizinga would seem to avoid the danger of imposing an alien conception onto different historical epochs and cultures, and so to stand forth as a model of historical objectivity. But he thereby falls into a second difficulty no less problematic to the historical approach generally.

According to the principle subsequently made famous by Wittgenstein, one best understands a given concept not by establishing an "essence" or essential definition (a "meaning") but by seeing how it and related concepts are used in a given culture (culture would here be Huizinga´s analogue to what Wittgenstein called "language games"). In so doing, one seems to gain a nicely empirical standpoint in which genuine objectivity would seem possible. But here is the problem; by this procedure, anything that is called play is play in that culture. The problems of an essentialist theory give way to the problems of a relativist one. There can be no possibility in principle of evaluating or criticizing a given culture´s conception of play except by an appeal to another culture´s conception, or, finally, to a transcultural conception of play, which is tantamount to a denial of the Wittgensteinian principle and a return to an essentialist position. Only by adhering to the Wittgensteinian relativist procedure, for example, is Huizinga able to insist upon close ties between play and war in culture after culture. Nowhere does he suggest (because his procedure will not allow him to suggest) that perhaps no matter how many cultures call war activities "play", it remains a perversion of genuine play. If there are such ties, say, in the Greek agon, then war was play for the ancient Greeks, notwithstanding the fact that one of that culture´s greatest spokesmen argued that in fact play was the opposite of war.[9] There are, then, two decisive dimensions to the issue of play which Huizinga´s historical method makes it impossible for him to consider: what I shall call the evaluative and the teleological dimensions.

To take the first: Huizinga´s "Wittgensteinian" method makes each culture´s conception of play (or of anything else) incorrigible. A culture cannot be wrong about what play is, since what play is is determined by the way that culture uses the notion. Much less can a culture have a perverse understanding of play. If a specific society considers activities which are cruel, demeaning, perhaps even murderous, to be play, we cannot say that its view of play is perverse save by appeal, again, to a transcultural conception. But do we not need to do precisely this? That is at least a legitimate question. I shall presently argue that the issue of value in play is exceedingly complex, that whether there is "good" and "bad" play, or whether only "good" play is authentic play, or whether play is "beyond good and evil", are questions both decisive to an understanding of play and immensely complex and important in themselves and in their consequences. But they cannot even be raised, much less answered, by Huizinga's historical approach.

Second and evidently related to the first problem is what I have called the teleological dimension of play. It is one thing to describe a culture's conception of play accurately and "objectively". But is play a concept which can be adequately encompassed, adequately understood, adequately appreciated, by even the most comprehensive <u>description</u> of a culture's -- or even of all cultures' -- <u>uses</u> of the concept? Do we not have to raise the teleological question, what <u>ought</u> our play to be like? If so, and I shall presently argue that this is indeed needful, then we have again come to the limits of the historical approach: it cannot in its own terms so much as raise this question. Description, whether historical or phenomenological, which does not or cannot raise teleological questions of phenomena shot through with teleological implications, is necessarily and radically incomplete.

As with the examination of the previous approaches, so here, what we have accomplished if we have succeeded is a critique, an establishing of some of the boundaries or limits of the historical approach followed by Huizinga. This in no way suggests that the approach should be abandoned or that its insights into the history of play are not of great value. The positon need not and should not be abandoned or denigrated; but it must be transcended, if we are to raise the questions which I have just suggested need to be raised. As it happens, and this is a complex conceptual issue in itself, the standpoint which can raise these questions and other questions left unasked by the previous approaches is the very standpoint from which I have been examining these other approaches by way of a critique. We are ready to take up a philosophical understanding of play.

Footnotes, Chapter 3

1). Huizinga, Johan, _Homo Ludens: A Study of the Play Element in Culture_, Boston, Beacon Press, 1950, Forward.
2). Ibid, page 3.
3). Ibid.
4). Ibid.
5). Ibid, page 4,
6). Ibid, page 3.
7). Ibid, page 90 ff.
8). Ibid, page 30 ff.
9). Plato, _Laws VII_, 803ff.

PART II

Chapter 4: The Stance of Play[1]

One might well ask why a turn to a philosophical account of play is even necessary after the preceding chapters. After all, having admitted that each of the preceding standpoints does contribute insight into play, perhaps all that is necessary is a summation of their cumulative insights in order to achieve the comprehensive account which we hold as an ideal. Moreover, since by almost any account, the philosophical standpoint will be less, not more empirical than the previous positions, is it not equally likely that any insights a philosophical approach might offer will have already been comprehended by the former approaches? In short, what in principle can a philosophic account of play hope to add to the cumulative insights of the previous positions? There are at least two responses I wish to make.

First, I would say that the philosophic standpoint is more fundamental than the others. To put the point more technically, the other standpoints are "ontic" standpoints (employing loosely Heidegger's use of the term) and will in every case yield only ontic responses, however correct and fruitful they happen to be. That is, each of the previous standpoints treats its object of investigation precisely as an object of investigation, even and especially human beings. As such, they in each case already assume a fundamental decision about the being of the entity being examined, namely, that it is an entity, an object, which can be appropriately examined by the methods of the sciences, which in every case assume that the object of study is a "thing". In the case of interest to us, when human beings and their behavior is studied by sociology, or psychology, or history, or any of the social sciences, just in so far as they apply techniques and methodologies derived from the natural sciences they already have decided at least this much about the being of human being, that human beings are things, objects, not in principle dissimilar from the other objects investigated by the natural sciences. This is what Heidegger means by the "ontic" character of these investigations. Obviously, then, there is a prior investigation necessary which will open up to question the being of what is being investigated, will ask after the nature of human beings who play. This questioning of the being of human being I call an ontological issue.

43

If we are to hope for or even aim for anything like comprehensiveness, we would need in addition to the most vast array of ontic information an ontological account of play, which it is the office of philosophy to give. Let me explain with an example. Suppose we begin with a specific question, one resolvable by appeal to ontic explanations. Suppose the question is, why is John, or Jane, who are normally pragmatic, serious, reasonable citizens, so attracted to play? Upon due investigation, the sociologist responds with an answer derived from the assumptions of that discipline. Let us say that John plays basketball because he is an urban black, for whom "the city game" has become one of the chief modes of social advancement, and that Jane plays golf because she comes from an upper class environment where golf is as much a social as an athletic skill. The psychologist adds that John needs an outlet for his intense aggression, yet one which preserves his need for belonging to a group: the teamwork and contact of basketball thus both reveal and help alleviate his psychological problems. Jane, on the other hand, whose family background is such that she has developed the sense that she can trust no one, plays golf because she is "on her own" there and not dependent on what for her seems the always undependable cooperation of others. The historian fills this out with an account of the historical development of the games involved and what, if any, connections they have to the respective cultures (black and Anglo-Saxon) from which the two people come. Now suppose, in addition, that all the information tendered by these three representatives is utterly correct. It would still be appropriate to ask, what is human being, that one needs to express aggressiveness (in play or elsewhere), that one needs both to feel a sense of belonging with others yet also a sense of autonomy, that the issue of trust would become thematic in one's life? Indeed, the specific answers offered lead almost naturally to these further questions, questions which are literally ontological, in that they ask after the being of human being. They are the kinds of questions to which I hope to respond in this and the following chapters.

Second, there is a self-referential basis for the importance of a philosophic account. The very enterprise in which we have been involved so far, the asking after the first principles and the boundaries or limits of various disciplines, has been since

44

Aristotle a peculiarly philosophic enterprise. The practicing psyhologist gives psychological accounts of play; he does not, qua psychologist, ask the kinds of questions of his own discipline which would constitute a critique thereof. So too with the other disciplines. That too is the office of philosophy. But philosophy has the peculiarity that it, and perhaps it alone of the various disciplines, is self-referential. In addition to asking critical (in the technical sense) questions of the other disciplines, it asks the same questions of itself, and does so qua philosophy. Again, to aim for comprehensiveness in one´s account of play demands a philosophical approach in addition to the approaches of the specific disciplines.

So a philosophical account is necessary. But what kind of philosophic account? Ideally, one which would respond to both the conditions discussed. That is, I want to ask after what play is that it appeals so much to human being as human, and at the same time to make my account self-referential. I want to ask after the stance of play.

Let me explain in detail what I mean by the "stance" of play. One way to begin is to indicate that I am here more interested in clarifying the intentional than the extensional characteristics of play. Later I will turn to a discussion of some extensional characteristics, especially as they may relate to the project of "defining" play; here it is the intentional dimension that interests me. When we play, we seem to have a certain orientation toward those with whom we play, toward our play equipment, toward time, space, indeed toward the world, which is distinctive. It is a mode of comportment toward things, a mode of being-in-the-world, which, although not utterly peculiar, is nevertheless different from our mode of comportment when we consider ourselves not to be playing. This orientation, mode of comportment, way of being, I call the stance of play. I want now to illuminate some of its distinctive characteristics, so that we may reflect on both its similarities to and differences from our "normal" or everyday stances. Consider the following experiential contrasts:

Scene I: I am going to work in the morning after a snowfall. I am forced to drive more slowly than usual and so I must get up earlier than I wish. The slow driving and the traffic jams that ensue make me

45

frustrated. When I park my car I must slog through
the already dirty snow to my office. It makes me cold
and wet. I try to resist all this by ignoring the
snow as much as possible. It is, for me, to use
Sartre's apt term, a "not".

Scene II: I am skiing. As I glide down the
mountain I must be especially aware of the minute
changes in the quality of the snow, for subtle
differences in the snow will elicit different
movements and positions of my body. Skiers have even
developed a vocabulary for these variations: powder,
packed powder, hard packed, loose granular, blue ice.
Nor is my sensitivity directed only on the snow. The
trees, which I had hardly noticed on the way to work,
now function in at least three ways for my
consciousness: as objects of beauty which I
occasionally pause to contemplate, as guides which
show me the way down the trail, and as threats which I
must carefully avoid as I wend my way through them
down the mountain.[2]

Or alternatively, Scene III: This time I am
taking the subway home from work. It is rush hour and
the streets, stations, and subway cars are mobbed.
People are passing me everywhere -- in front of me,
behind me, alongside me. In the subway car we are
pressed up against each other so tightly that we
hinder each other's movements. I deal with this
uncomfortable situation, again, by ignoring it as much
as possible. I try to read the newspaper.

Scene IV: People are also passing behind me, in
front of me, alongside me, occasionally against me,
hindering my movement. But this time I am on a
basketball court, and my whole attention is directed
to being fully aware of the movements of everyone, my
teammates and opposition alike. I dribble slowly
toward my teammate, who pretends to come toward me but
suddenly cuts behind the man defending him toward the
basket. I anticipate this and pass the ball to where
he will soon be, watching out of the corner of my eye
that none of the opposing players have also
anticipated the play and are moving to intercept the
pass. Another successful "back-door" play! Again, it
is not just the other players to which my heightened
sensitivity is directed. I notice the relative
resilience of the floor and backboard, to which I
adjust my dribbling and shooting, and, although this
often seems remarkable to the uninitiated, if the

46

ten-foot high basket were as much as an inch high or
low, the other players and I would surely notice it.

    With due apologies for the quality of the drama,
I suggest that such contrasts, and hundreds of others
like them, are reasonably accurate and common.   In
each pair, one situation is usually characterized as
play, the other not. Taking them as paradigms, then,
of play and non-play, I now ask what is different
about the stance taken toward our experience in the
two play situations, what distinguishes it from the
stances taken in the non-playful encounters.

    To begin, I note that in the play situations I am
called upon, or call upon myself, to have a heightened
sense of openness toward my surroundings.   While
skiing, I must be far more aware that I usually am of
subtle variations in the quality of the snow, the
steepness of the slopes, the location of trees and
other people. While playing basketball, I am called
upon to be constantly open to, aware of, the location
and movements of the respective players, the
resilience of the floor and backboard, the size of the
court, and whatever possibilities open up in the game
as a result. Clearly, then, the play situations seem
to demand an openness to my environment not called for
in the non-playful situations. Let us say, then, that
one notable characteristic of the stance of play is
openness.

    But openness is not the whole of the distinction.
It is hardly sufficient while skiing simply to be open
to the various nuances I mentioned, to take notice, as
it were, and leave it at that. Rather, I have to be
capable of responding to that openness in a way called
for by the situation, and my success as a skier
depends in good measure on my capacity to respond
appropriately to each developing situation.
Similarly, I would be a poor basketball player --
indeed, I could hardly consider myself to be playing
basketball -- if I merely noticed with extraordinary
sensitivity the various movements of the players.
Again, my success as a player, even my very status as
a player, demands that I respond as best I can to
whatever possibilities my openness to the game
elicits. Responsiveness, then could be called a
second "moment" in the stance of play, a second
decisive characteristic of our orientation toward
things exhibited in the two play situations.

47

Now I am aware that two instances do not make a
sound inductive generalization. Nevertheless, I
boldly suggest that other examples one may choose will
reveal the same structure present in typical play
situations and present to a far lesser degree in
non-play situations, a structure which I shall call
responsive openness, the meaning of which I hope I
have made initially clear above. It holds, for
example, for children playing house, for a hike in the
wilderness, for a person fishing along a quiet stream,
for someone playing the guitar, as well as for the
standard games usually considered play. I would add
that responsiveness and openness together are what
bring about the well-known experience of immersion,
the sense we often have in play of being totally
involved in our activity, not abstracted or distanced
in any way from what we are doing. This immersion,
which is so often part of the appeal of play, is in
significant measure a function of our capacity, when
we take the stance of play, to be at once more open to
our situation and more responsive to it. This sense
of totality, here of the totality of one's involvement
in an activity, always appeals to us finite humans,
and the reasons why must be considered subsequently.
Here the points to be made are that play is one of
those phenomena where we again and again achieve that
sense of totality, that intimation of completeness,
and that the possibility of its doing so is grounded
in the very stance of play itself, which I have called
responsive openness.

Already, however, a few points of clarification
are needed. First, it should be clear that the
interpretation of play as the stance of responsive
openness does not admit of a rigid dichotomy between
playful and unplayful activities, but rather places
them on a continuum. It might be observed, for
example, that anyone who is merely conscious is at
least minimally open and at least minimally responsive
to an environment. Thus what I have in mind is a
matter of degree. There are times in our lives,
situations we experience, stances that we from time to
time take, in which we are more responsively open than
others. Play is one of those situations and stances
wherein we are most responsively open, and this is one
of its distinctive possibilities.

This leads to a second point. It should be clear
now that mine is an intentional rather than an
extensional conception of play. I see no way on my

48

view definitively to delineate that a, b, and c specific activities, e.g. skiing, basketball, and tennis, are and are always play, wereas x, y, and z specific activities, e.g. going to or from work, doing the dishes, or running for president, are not play. Rather, as the term "stance" implies, this view has to do with the "intention", comportment, or orientation of the putative player towards the activity. This enables us to understand a well-known phenomenon such as the following: two people may be exhibiting the same sort of behavior, hitting a ball over a net with a racquet in the general direction of the other person who tries to hit it back. Yet suppose we happen to know that one of them participates in tennis in the mode of compulsion. He begins the day by working himself into a hatred of his opponent. He gets furious at all close line calls that are not in his favor. He pounds his racquet in anger at his own mistakes. The two are engaging in the same activity, indeed;, but, we may say, only one of them is truly playing tennis. Play, that is, has more to do with our stance toward a given activity than with the specific behavioral details of the activity itself. This is of course compatible, as I hope to show, with the view that certain specific activities, such as basketball or skiing, may be more conducive to the taking of the play stance than others, such as fighting a war or standing in an unemployment line. Certain activities thus may invite the stance of responsive openness (though not guarantee it) whereas others may tend to preclude it.

Considerations such as these lead me to emphasize that in characterizing play as responsive openness I do not intend to offer it as a formal "definition" of play. Some of the best philosophical analysis in the area of play and sport has centered around the controversy regarding the possibility of definition.[3] Can successful definitions be offered of "game", "play", or "sport"? Or, following a Wittgensteinian inclination, are such efforts foredoomed, and can we at best hope for a series of "family resemblances"? Can a definitive distinction be maintained between "game", "sport", and "athletics"? Or again, are there merely shades of difference here which will vary with the historical and even colloquial variations in usage of the terms? To repeat, fascinating as this controversy sometimes is, I wish to deny that with my characterization of play as responsive openness I enter it as a candidate for a definition. For one thing, once I entered that "language game", I would be subject to its rules and limitations; my "definition" would be immediately identified as "too broad" -- including within its domain such "non-playful" activities as guarding the president or being a traffic control officer at a large airport -- and possibly even "too narrow" -- insofar as it tends to exclude certain participants in activities usually considered "play", such as the misguided tennis player of a previous example. Such considerations would indeed dispense with responsive openness as a definition of play, but not, I wish to argue, as a fruitful if partial characterization of what I have called the stance of play. To repeat a formulation from my introduction, my project is in no sense to "solve" the problem of play -- as a successful definition might be supposed to do -- but rather reflectively to clarify our experience of play. At least one decisive difference between the two projects is this: reflective clarification does not seek, and so of course does not achieve, the kind of closure sought and achieved by successful "definitions". For my purposes, then, the obvious overlap between occasions of responsive openness which seem to be playful and those that do not will become an issue for further reflection rather than a refutation of a putative definition. But first, we must consider further the ontological status of play as a "stance" toward things which we from time to time achieve.

Earlier, I suggested that the notion of play as a stance of responsive openness is more primordial than even the most accurate psychological, sociological, or historical accounts of play. Why, we need now to ask, should this be so? I suggest that play as responsive openness achieves such primordiality, and therefore that play is such a primary human phenomenon, because this stance is directly grounded in, and so flows from, the nature of human being itself, or at least a certain conception of human being which I would espouse. For this reason, a genuine understanding of the stance of play, of what it is and of its appeal to human being, can only be won through a consideration of human being itself and of how play has its origin in that being. What then is that conception of human being which I would espouse and what are its most significant alternatives?

It has been said by many a philosopher that human being or human nature is a paradox.[4] Indeed, the case

has been argued at great length. If the term
"paradox" is an exaggeration, it is only slightly so.
For any attempt to think about the nature of human
being confronts before long a series of at least
contrary tendencies, tensions, which can very easily
seem paradoxical. Let me now cite only a few of what
I hope will be the most fundamental ways in which this
tendency gets exhibited. Each of them, as we shall
see, bears on the stance of play as responsive
openness.

The first apparent paradox has to do with the
human tendency to vacillate between an experience of
incompleteness or partiality and the experience of
wholeness, of an overflowing overfullness. Both
experiences need elaboration.

We experience ourselves, again and again, as
incomplete, as beings who lack, and as a consequence,
who desire wholeness. This syndrome seems to contain
three "moments". First is what we might call the
ontological moment. We are, we have our being, as
incomplete, partial, in an indefinite variety of ways.
There is an ontological negativity about human beings;
we are not autonomous. Our lives are characterized by
an apparently ever-expanding variety of needs, all of
which testify to our lacks. But already in this is
implicit the second moment. We <u>experience</u> that
incompleteness; we are conscious of it, even if only
vaguely. Indeed, the most self-conscious among us
<u>recognize</u> our lacks as such, we understand something
of what it is that we lack. Third and decisively, as
we experience and recognize our lacks, we strive to
overcome them. We have in us an impetus, a drive,
which moves us to seek fulfillment. Thus, for
example, I may experience an incompleteness of wealth,
and try to overcome it by making a fortune in
business, or an incompleteness of political power,
which I seek to overcome by running for public office.
I may experience a lack of self-expression, which I
seek to overcome by creating works of art, or
decisively, I may experience a lack of wisdom, which I
can only overcome by becoming a philosopher. It is
important to note the implication here: this triadic
syndrome of incompleteness, recognition thereof, and
striving to overcome it contributes to what each of us
<u>is</u>. Are you an athlete, artist, wife, and mother? If
so, these attest to the ways in which you have
experienced partiality and tried to overcome it.

51

But this incompleteness syndrome is only one side of the story, and here the first of the apparent paradoxes enters. Many times, indeed in the very midst of striving to overcome experienced incompleteness, we also experience a kind of wholeness, more than that, a kind of over-fullness and over-flowing, in which, as we say, we ex-press ourselves (note the literal meaning here: "to press out"). We pour out something of ourselves, almost as a gift, to someone or to the world. Of all the human experiences, perhaps love and friendship are the most obvious instances of this co-presence of incompleteness and overflowing. Our love for another is founded in and attests to our lack, but it is at once a giving of ourselves, a gift of the abundance of what we are.

That play as responsive openness is founded in this aspect of our natures can now be made clear. Suppose, to the contrary of what I have said, that we were characterized neither by incompleteness nor by that overflowing overfullness which leads us to pour out ourselves. Suppose we were simply complete, that we "are what we are and not another thing". We would then not be called upon to be open, since, lacking nothing, we would need to be open to nothing. Nor, lacking the impetus of overflowing, would we be responsive, in so far as a response is just such an outpouring or ex-pressing of ourselves. Responsive openness, then, is founded in and itself is an expression of our natures as incomplete/overfull. Or, play is a natural consequence of what it means to be human.

The second of the apparently paradoxical characterizations of human nature may be somewhat more controversial, since many have argued exclusively in behalf of one or the other side of the paradox. But I shall argue, again, that we are both. I refer to the interpretation of human being as by nature monadic or nuclear, and, on the other hand, the understanding of human being as fundamentally relational. There have been many spokesmen for both separately, as well as monumental efforts to hold them together, however precariously, in a single human nature.

According to the monadic or nuclear view of human being, we are to be understood as autonomous, independent beings, "monads", who to be sure may from time to time enter into relations with others, but

52

whose essential natures are not informed by those relations. This is not a view which argues that the culmination of human being is to become a hermit. But it does argue that our nature is constituted by factors to which our relations with others, positive or negative, are extrinsic.[5] Typically, spokesmen for this view emphasize the place of autonomy, of independence, and, to use the language of certain existentialist thinkers, of "authenticity" (the German word is instructive here: Eighentlichkeit is rooted in Eigen, "own". Eigentlichkeit is the state of "being one's own"). In turn, this view can be stated descriptively (the way human beings are is monadic, whether we like this situation or not) or it can be stated teleologically (the way human beings are at their best is monadic, just insofar as they overcome an inferior state of essential involvement with or dependence on others). In our philosophical tradition, perhaps Nietzsche to an extent and Kierkegaard have been the outstanding spokesmen for the latter view. For Kierkegaard, what he called "the category of the individual" was a state to be achieved out of an involvement with others and as a sine qua non of genuinely becoming a Christian. Kierkegaard emphasized the monadic character of this individual:

> "I bind myself to make every man whom I can include in the category 'the individual' into a Christian, or rather, since no man can do that for another, I vouch for his becoming one. As 'that individual' he is alone, alone in the whole world, alone----before God."[6]

Similarly, Nietzsche sometimes regards the status of monadic individuality as an achievement out of what he sardonically calls "the herd", who need each other essentially. For example, in Thus Spake Zarathustra, speaking against what he calls the "spirit of gravity", Zarathustra says,

> "But whoever would become light and a bird must love himself: thus I teach. Not, to be sure, with the love of the wilting and waiting: for among those even self-love stinks. One must learn to love oneself -- thus I teach -- with a wholesome and healthy love, so that one can be with oneself and need not roam. Such roaming

baptizes itself ´love of the neighbor´;
with this phrase the best lies and
hypocricies have been perpetrated so far,
and especially by such as were a grave
burden for all the world."[7]

Thus Nietzsche, like Kierkegaard, at times affirms in
perhaps its most radical form the monadic conception
of the individual, and does so in such a way as to
explicitly repudiate as inferior a "relationalism"
which he interprets as inauthentic, as "herd
mentality", the work of the "spirit of gravity".

This understanding seems particularly appealing
to Americans as part of our self-image as a "frontier
people" whose paradigmatic members leave behind "the
many" and head into the wilderness to "make it on
own´s own". Henry David Thoreau is a popular
spokesman for this conception. But this view is also
stated descriptively as simply the way human beings
are. Monadic individualism, for example, is evidently
the view underlying the economic system of capitalism
so dominant in the world today. This is seen perhaps
most easily by reference to Adam Smith´s The Wealth of
Nations, the foundational theoretical treatise on
capitalism. There self-interest and competition are
clearly seen as central assumptions of the system.
Indeed, when Smith is moved to defend the claim that
capitalism will help not just isolated individuals who
succeed but society as a whole, he invokes what he
calls "the invisible hand", teaching -- or hoping --
that monadic individuals, motivated by self-interest
entirely, with no altruistic interest whatsoever, will
nevertheless, by a happy accident, bring about a
better condition for all. Thus even his attempted
assertion of a general benefit is founded on a monadic
individualism.

More generally, the appeal of this conception of
the individual is familiar to us all. The well-known
"identity crisis" could be interpreted as the
painfully experienced absence of this individuality.
None of us like being "too dependent" on others. Even
in those experiences which would seem essentially
relational, such as love, we are all troubled when
such relations become ones of dependency.[8] The
appeal, then, of this conception of the individual
should be clear.

But no more so than its apparent opposite, which I have called the relational view. According to this view, our relations with other people or with the world are not just something into which we from time to time enter. They are rather essential to our very natures. Many of the very words we employ to name who we are -- husband, father, teacher, philosopher -- are names of relations with other people or things. Just as with the monadic view, this position has been asserted sometimes as a descriptive, sometimes as a teleological account. Of the latter, perhaps the most famous and influential spokesman in our tradition is Karl Marx. Marx's doctrine of "species being" is his version of the view that human beings are as relational. But species being is not so much a description of the way things are -- especially under capitalism -- but of the way they ought to be and will be under the proper economic conditions. Indeed, part of the core of Marx's critique of capitalism is that it is founded on a conception of the individual which, though descriptively true under capitalism, is teleologically defective. For example, in the Judenfrage, in a critique of the supposed "right to property", Marx says,

> "The right of property is therefore the right to enjoy one's fortune and to dispose of it as one will; without regard for other men and independently of society. It is the right of self-interest. This individual liberty, and its application, form the basis of civil society. It leads every man to see in other men, not the realization, but rather the limitation of his own liberty.....The term 'equality' here has no political significance. It is only the equal right to liberty as defined above; namely that every man is equally regarded as a self-sufficient monad...None of the supposed rights of man, therefore, go beyond the egoistic man, man as he is, as a member of civil society; that is, an individual separated from the community, withdrawn into himself, wholly preoccupied with his private interest and acting in accordance with his private caprice. Man is far from being considered, in the rights of man, as a species-being."[9]

Again, with more conciseness, Marx's sixth of the twelve "Theses On Feuerbach" says:

> "Feuerbach resolves the religious essence
> into the <u>human</u> essence. But the human
> essence is no abstraction inherent in each
> single individual. In reality it is the
> ensemble of the social relations."[10]

However, the same relational conception of the individual has also been stated as a description of the way human beings in fact are. One could point to Aristotle's famous "definition" of human being as "the political animal", or in our own century to perhaps the most explicit statement of this view in our entire tradition, that of Martin Buber at the beginning of his seminal work, I <u>And</u> <u>Thou</u>:

> "There is no I taken by itself, but only
> the I of the primary word I-thou and the
> I of the primary word I-it."[11]

As with the monadic, the relational view of human being has long had strong appeal. The view that we fulfill ourselves with and through others, that we become who we can be through our involvements with others, is as old as the Dionysian ecstasy, as enduring as the phenomenon of nationalism, and as recent as a contemporary coach's exhortation to his players in behalf of teamwork.

So stated, the two appear to be opposed conceptions of human being, and as I have indicated, they have often been presented as such. Nevertheless, because of the evident appeal of both, many of the greatest thinkers in our tradition have attempted to hold the two views together, however precariously, in a unity, and they have done so out of a conviction that only thus could they be true to the nature of things, that however paradoxical it may seem, human beings are both monadic and relational. Thinkers as diverse as Plato, Hegel, Kant, Rousseau, Schleirmacher, and the poet William Blake have clearly been motivated by such an understanding. As but one particularly succinct example I quote from Kant's work, <u>Idea</u> <u>for</u> <u>a</u> <u>Universal</u> <u>History</u> <u>with</u> <u>a</u> <u>Cosmopolitan</u> <u>Intent</u>:

"I mean by antagonism (in society) the
asocial sociability of man, i.e. the
propensity of men to enter into a society,
which propensity is, however, linked to a
constant mutual resistance which threatens
to dissolve this society. This propensity
is apparently innate in man. Man has an
inclination to associate himself, because
in such a state he feels himself more like
a man, capable of developing his natural
faculties. Man also has a marked propensity
to isolate himself, because he finds in
himself the asocial quality to want to arrange
everything according to his own ideas."[12]

Now as this quote indicates, these thinkers
maintain the co-presence of both conceptions not out
of a love of paradox but out of a conviction that only
this is true to human being. I would like to add at
least to the plausibility of this conviction by noting
that there is a genuine coherence between this duality
of monadic/relational conceptions of human being and
the dualities discussed earlier, the
incompleteness/overfullness dimensions of human nature
and the understanding of play as responsive openness.

To begin with the connection to incompleteness
and overfullness, the monadic element of our nature
has a clear correspondence with the element of
completeness or overfullness. As monadic, we think of
ourselves as embodying a kind of completeness. We
are, or seek to be, independent, self-reliant. When
we do enter into relations with others, that relation
flows not from our need but from our overfullness; it
is a gift of ourselves that we give. Nietzsche's
Zarathustra is an exemplar of this understanding of
the individual.[13] Conversely, the relational
conception is commensurate with our self-understanding
as incomplete beings. As relational, because we take
on the being that is ours in and through our relations
with others, we reveal ourselves as incomplete; we do
not contain within ourselves the ingredients of
completeness. The incompleteness/overfullness and
relational/monadic understandings of the individual
could be said to be co-primordial and reflective of
each other. No wonder, then, that both appear as
tensions, even paradoxes.

No wonder, either, that play as responsive openness also can be seen as founded in our bi-fold nature as monadic and relational. Our openness to things, to others, is a consequence of our relationality. If we were utterly monadic, like Leibniz's monads we would have no "windows" to the world, no need for openness to others. Our essential relationality calls for our orientation toward others in the mode of openness, so that we may fulfill our natures. Our responsiveness, in turn, flows from our overfullness, and so from what we are "in ourselves". The expression of our responsiveness may or may not result in a relation with others; but it's source, again, is in what we are in ourselves, and so in our natures as monadic. Responsiveness is the word for this flowing out of our monadic natures to the world, this gift, and in a sense, this re-turn to others. Responsive openness thus flows from our double natures as monadic and relational at once. Again, we play by nature.

A third duality, to which responsive openness stands in perhaps the most intimate, if precarious, connection, could be called the tension of dominance and submission. These are to be understood not so much as aspects of human being per se, but rather, like responsive openness itself, as two stances toward the world and other people, stances which throughout our tradition have been appealed to and recommended as the best comportment toward others. Because it has been the most pervasive and visible, let me begin with the stance of dominance.

For my purposes, the stance of dominance has two fundamental cultural facets, the effort to "master nature" and the attitude of dominance towards our fellow human beings, nowadays usually accorded the designation "alienation," the ubiquitousness of which can be gleaned from a perusal of contemporary treatises on politics, economics, sociology, psychology, youth, race-relations, women, and certainly sports. The attitude toward nature is perhaps best exhibited in the close relation that has been preserved since the 17th century beginnings of modern science between it and the mastery of nature. One can find in Descartes, Galileo, Bacon, Machiavelli, or again in Vico or Kant, explicit statements that reveal that they considered the project of modern science to be inseparable from the experience of nature as an enemy which we must either conquer or by whom we will continue to be victimized.[14] This view continues to punctuate the vocabulary of science and of technology to this day. As a recent poignant example, I would point to the speeches and comments which accompanied the landing of the first men on the moon, surely one of our most spectacular scientific and technological achievements. Again and again, commentators spoke of our "mastery" of the forces of nature, of our future "conquests" of outer space and other planets, even of the so-called "peaceful" uses to which the knowledge gained could be put, such as the "control" of our environment and the making of more comfortable and "secure" lives for us all. Few noted that midst our insistence on other fronts that we were interested only in peace and reconciliation between nations, the language used to describe this most spectacular scientific achievement was almost exclusively the vocabulary of war. Even the way in which we commonly refer to the fruits of the earth as "natural resources" suggests the element of exploitation which is our basic attitude toward nature, the dubious rewards of which are now becoming manifest in such phenomena as the ecological crisis, massive pollution of all sorts, and most recently, the depletion of fuel deposits and ensuing political tensions that accompany it. Let it suffice to say, then, that the close connection which the 17th century founders saw and articulated between the development of science and the mastery of a nature construed as our enemy has by no means been mitigated in our contemporary understanding.

On the level of human relations, the dominance of the stance of dominance is at least as obvious. We are fond of congratulating ourselves that we have left behind perhaps the most blatant manifestation of this stance known to mankind, the institution of slavery. But that we have only made more subtle and rhetorically acceptable the dominion of this stance can be seen, as noted above, by the ubiquitousness of the experience of alienation in modern culture. It is instructive, for example, that more and more of the relations between people and nations, on the political, economic, and social level, are construed not, e.g. as "justice" relations, but as "power relations". Every interest group that experiences the brunt of alienated power and attempts to escape its yoke invariably adopts as its slogan a reference to power desired. We thus hear of "black power," "female power," "student power" etc. Movements do not rally

59

under what in a bygone era would have been considered the more legitimate banner of "black justice," or "feminine justice," etc. Even the ideal of democracy, an ideal at least as old as ancient Athens, has in our time received a novel and revealing formulation: power to the people. In the area of human relations, then, the stance of dominance continues to hold sway to a remarkable, not to say depressing, degree.

But there is another stance toward the world and other people that from time to time has played a significant role in our culture, a stance which may well be understood as the converse of the stance of dominance, adopted and recommended often by those who are unsuccessful at the project of dominance. I have called this the stance of submission. Philosophically, it is present in those views which emphasize the extent to which we must accept our place in the movement of history, a movement in which we unwittingly participate but which is finally outside of our control. We are told to accept "an idea whose time has come" because it has come, or as it is often put in the less technical but more colorful language of culture, "it's what's happening, baby" — usually asserted as a reason for accepting some phenomenon or other. Again we have existential philosophers telling us that we must "await" in silence the uncanny voice of being, that the most recent Seinsgeschick must be accepted because it is a happening of being. As the Beatles put a similar point in their own inimitable way, "Speaking words of wisdom, let it be." It is fair to say that this stance of submission is dominant in the widespread and much imitated flower child element of the hippie culture, not to speak of its more deplorable consequences for the so-called drug-culture. But it can also arise out of a positive and, at least in its intentions, praiseworthy effort not to impose arbitrary values, constructs, or interpretations on things, not to engage in "cultural imperialism" for example, but rather to let things and other people be "as they are". This stance can often bring with it a sense of comfort, peace, and acceptability in a world otherwise out of joint, a point which was recognized and developed in oriental thinking long before it became popular in the west. The stance of submission, then, could be said to work in a kind of dialectic with the stance of dominance, so that together they hold a virtual hegemony over our cultural experience.

60

Once again, it is not difficult to see a connection between the dominance/submission duality and the aforementioned dualities of incompleteness/overfullness, monadic/relational, and most decisively, play as responsive openness. The stance of dominance, first of all, could be understood as a kind of radicalized overfullness, one unmoderated by incompleteness. Similarly, submission is an extreme form of incompleteness, where the passivity implicit in the word testifies to a lack of that overflowing overfullness which might lead toward dominance. From a different perspective, we might understand the urge to dominance as a consequence of our incompleteness (we "overcome" a perceived threat) and submission as a mode of completeness, however peculiar. The point of correlation between the two dualities would remain. Again, though here I think the connection is less rigorous, we can easily associate the stance of dominance with a radicalized monadic individualism, notwithstanding that dominance or mastery is, after all a certain kind of relation. Hegel, in the famous master/slave dialectic of <u>The Phenomenology</u> of <u>Spirit</u>, makes this point with great penetration, showing both how such monadic indpendence arises and how it disintegrates into its opposite.[15] Submission, in turn, is more essentially relational just insofar as such submission implies a passive dependence on the other.

But the most powerful and important connection is between the dominance/submission duality and the stance of play understood as responsive openness. Here we must make more explicit an asymmetry between responsive openness and dominance/submission, namely, that dominance and submission are opposites, whereas I am arguing that play is just the co-presence, however tenuous, of responsiveness and openness. Nevertheless, there is a decisive relation between them. If we think of the stances of dominance and submission as polar extremes, we can see responsive openness as in the middle between them, almost in the manner of an Aristotelian mean. Responsive openness, that is, occupies a precarious balance between dominance and submission in such a way that an excess of responsiveness easily devolves into dominance, an excessive openness into submission. An example should make my point clear. Return to the example of the basketball game used earlier. Suppose that instead of preserving the balance of responsiveness and openness there suggested, my responses became increasingly strong, domineering, and I became less and less open to possibilities of the game. Several things are likely. I will probably fail to see many of the openings my teammates may make, and thus cease to be as integral a participant in the game. More strongly, my excessive responsiveness is likely to emerge, given the physical nature of the game, as an alienating attempt _really_ to "beat" my opposition; I may get into a fight, at which time, as we often say, the game falls apart, we are no longer playing. Generally, then, the all too common talk about "killing the opposition", hurting opponents, etc, is on my view a misconstrual of the very nature of play, it is literally to cease playing, to cease being responsively open.

Since most instances of play in our culture are founded on active response, it is difficult to think of examples of an excessive openness become submission which are not simply comic, but perhaps that is just as well. Consider yourself skiing down a mountain, becoming less and less responsive to the snow, trees, etc., more and more passively open. I daresay you will be picturing yourself lying down on the snow, the object of laughter from other skiers not so intoxicated with open-mindedness.

My point, I hope, is more clear. Play as responsive openness stands in a precarious balance between dominance and submission. Dominance moderated by openness becomes responsiveness. Submission moderated by responsiveness becomes openness. Held togther in a unity, they become the very spirit, the stance, of play. Understood in this way, play becomes not merely an idle pastime but an achievement precarious and difficult -- precarious because it exists as a tenuous balance of opposed possibilities, difficult because it must be achieved as a transcendence out of one or other stances which are themselves seductive and even inertial. At the same time, it can be seen to be natural in the teleological sense of that word: not the way we always are as an empirical matter but the way we are in so far as we adequately fulfill our natures.

But to invoke the issue of teleology is necessarily to invoke the issue of value, and so forces us to a consideration of the normative element in play. Consider the following, which might be offered as a possible objection to the earlier

62

examples upon which I developed my understanding of play as responsive openness: It is all very well to talk of people skiing or playing basketball, as opposed to people trudging through snow or taking the subway home from work, as exhibiting that stance of responsiveness and openness identified as the stance of play. Unfortunately for my case, however, there are other examples not so congenial to my point. I might, for example, have offered the following as an example of responsive openness:

Scene I: I am going home on the subway. The car is crowded with people pressing up against each other, but I am delighted by this, for I am a pick-pocket. My awareness of everything around me is heightened, for I must be open to whatever possibility presents itself. More than that, I must be capable of responding to any opportunity that arises. My stance is thus a paradigm of responsive openness.

Or alternatively,

Scene II: I am trudging down the street on my way to work through the snow. But I am exquisitely aware of everyone around me, and especially open to the appearance of a certain person. Moreover, when that person appears, I must be immediately responsive to that situation and the possibilities it presents. I, too, am a model of responsive openness. For I am a Mafia "hit-man", and I am about to eliminate the rival leader, Frederico, "Fat Freddy" Bombasto, who should be walking down the street any minute now.

For that matter, what of the control tower officials at an airport, or a neurological surgeon performing a delicate operation, a sculptor putting the finishing touches on a masterpiece, or a secret service agent guarding the president, a lion-tamer, or two lovers, engaged in that most exquisite of activities which exhibits both incompleteness and overflowing fulness, which calls most of all for responsive openness?

In order adequately to turn to the question of value in play, we must first take up a more obvious question, upon which I touched earlier in my insistence that responsive openness could not possibly be construed as a "definition" of play because it would be far too broad. Presumably, few people would consider all the above examples as instances of play.

All play may be responsive openness, but not all instances of responsive openness are play. More technically, in the stance of responsive openness I have perhaps discovered a necessary but not a sufficient condition for play. It is therefore tempting to ask, what other characteristics might one suggest which would distinguish playful from non-playful instances of responsive openness? But I ask this question with trepidation, because it once again runs the risk of reducing my reflective effort to that of "defining" play, which I have already insisted I do not intend to do. Nevertheless, with the disclaimer that a definition is not what I intend, I turn now to certain other characteristics which strike me as, like responsive openness itself, present in our play in a heightened or especially striking way. The first of these characteristics is finitude.

Perhaps the most obvious instance of finitude in play is one brought to light with special force in that class of play-phenomena which we call games. I refer to the oft-cited "rule-governed" character of games. It is true enough that in our games we accept the limitations imposed on our possibilities by rules in order to play the game.[16] Rigorously rule-governed games such as chess or the familiar children's game "giant steps" make this acceptance of limitation most obvious. But as Bernard Suits has pointed out, whereever we have games there are some rules and so some limitations, and moreover, the vast majority of those activities which we typically regard as play, even those especially "spontaneous" ones, are seen upon reflection to have at least some rules.[17] One of the differences between "adult" and "children's" games tends to be that adults adhere more rigorously to the established rules of a given game, whereas children seem much more willing to adjust rules to suit the situation, or even their whims. This does not deny, however, the presence of some element of rule, and so some recognition of the role of finitude in our play.

Of course, being rule-governed is no more a peculiar or distinguishing characteristic of games than is the stance of responsive openness. One might say that almost every mode of activity is governed by the presence of at least some sort of rules, laws, or conventions. The point is rather that in games, the rule-governed element and the finitude it entails is made an explicit theme of the activity itself. Our attention is called to the rules of a game in an especially powerful way as we play, and we are called upon to respond to and in the light of that finitude I know that one of the "rules" of life as a citizen is that I may not physically assault someone with whom I disagree. Rarely, however, is the presence of that rule as integral a part of my activity as is, for example, the rule when I am playing basketball that I must dribble the ball when I move with it rather than simply carry it. That rule "constitutes" the game, helps give it its meaning, in a far more manifest way that the more general rules of everyday activity. In so doing, the significance of rules, both positive and negative, is called to our attention.

A second manifestation of finitude, present throughout our lives but once again made thematic in our play, is our own bodily limitation. As embodied we are literally placed, situated. We are always in one place, and so we cannot be in all places. Moreover, the specific bodies that we have limit our possiblity even more; our size, our speed, our agility, our physical skill all are precisely tested in our play. In taking our bodies to their limits, we discover and recognize those limits with special force. As a person 5'8" tall, I do not usually experience myself as "small", my stature does not come home to me as limitation, until I step on a basketball floor with my taller colleagues. In running a long road race, or even in my daily "fun-runs", I am reminded of the limits of my bodily strength and endurance. Even in the freest, most spontaneous kinds of play, the finitude of embodiment comes clear; when a family engages in playful roughhousing, an unintended injury to someone or the eventual exhaustion of one or all, however satisfying, reminds us of our limitation. It must be acknowledged immediately that it is also in play that my bodily possibilities come to the fore; this issue will become thematic presently. Here I wish to emphasize that however exhilarating our experience of bodily possibility might be in play, it is also here that we experience in a powerful and direct way embodiment as limiting, as finitude.

There are two dimensions to this bodily limitation which deserve special mention: the finitude of space and the finitude of time. The finitude of space is perhaps clearest in those play activities which have delineated boundaries. In a

65

football game, the halfback cannot run outside of the sideline to avoid being tackled, and with a 250 lb. lineman bearing down on him, that can be awesome limitation indeed. But spatial limitation need not involve boundaries in a rigorously rule-governed game. A fisherman experiences such limitation poignantly as he stares at a beautiful pool, no doubt full of trout, but with so many overhanging branches that he cannot present his fly with which to tempt the fish.

The awareness of temporal limitation is similarly powerful in play. Again, more highly structured games are perhaps the clearest examples. In a basketball game of forty minutes, the limitations of time are felt with full force, especially on those occasions when one is trying to come from behind. Indeed, it is this increasing force of temporal finitude as the game moves toward an end that make the waning moments of a game so much more intense. A tie score in the first few minutes of the game is far less suspenseful than a tie with one minute left, and the reason is the impending presence of the end. But the significance of temporality in play by no means demands "clock time" such as a forty minute game. It is as present in a three-set tennis match or an eighteen-hole golf game, where "clock time", measured minutes, is not so critical a factor. This is no less so, to use a less structured example again, for our fisherman, whose "timing" must be right on every cast, and for whom the descending darkness tolls the immanent end of his day's quest. In all these cases as with the previous ones, the limitations of time, present always in our lives as a whole but more opaquely, are made thematic, integral in our play, and we are invited to acknowledge those limitations as such.

But part of what gets revealed about our finitude in play is that it is not mere limitation. The reverse side of finitude, as it were, is possibility.[18] The rules of games, which limit our moves, also make the game possible as the game that it is; to render finite is at once to de-fine, to grant meaning. My body, which limits me in so many ways, is my possibility, or better, my possibilities. My small stature among basketball players, limitation to be sure, is also my possibility. I am (or was!) quicker and more agile than the bigger players. My diminutiveness gives me a role to play. The activity of running, which may exhaust me and reveal my limitation, also allows me to celebrate my body, its

66

speed, its endurance, its health. My family's roughhouse sessions grant us a playful, exhuberant, physical encounter not to be missed. The same is true with the limitations of spatiality. The boundaries of the football field offer the place of the game. Only within and in terms of those boundaries does the game take on meaning and become the game that it is. What would a football game be like with no sidelines and no goals? The spatial limitations in fishing make it the challenge that it is, allow it, invite it, to become play, long after it is easier and more economical to buy our fish at the store. With temporality, once again, the limits imposed by the time of a game also grant it meaning. Most of us have had the experience of playing a sand-lot game where, after a long time, the score is forgotten; far from "freeing" the game from the "limits" of time, the game soon dissipates. We need the context of meaning which our temporal finitude grants.

It is also in the finitude of our play that the phenomenon of immersion, to which I earlier alluded, is located. Immersion is a function of intense focus, and finitude, limitation, is the context wherein intense focus is possible. If one can imagine an infinite consciousness, one could also imagine it having a capacity for total immersion in the whole. But because we are not infinite but finite, we can only immerse ourselves in finite projects. The broader, more diffuse those projects, the less our capacity for genuine immersion. We all know this as the experience of trying to concentrate on too much at once. Yet strange as it seems, this finitude also makes it possible for us to achieve within that finite context that exhilarating and fulfilling experience of immersion and intimation of totality usually unavailable to us in the broader and more diffuse context of the everyday. In playing a specific game, with specific rules, for a specific length of time and within specific boundaries, I can and sometimes do immerse myself totally, and thereby experience a totality rarely available to me otherwise. This too is a distinctive possibility of the finitude of play.

What is this strange intimacy between finitude and possibility which we discover so clearly in our play? Insofar as our possibility is co-extensive with our freedom, we can say that in play is exhibited a conception of freedom by no means reducible to the model of omnipotence -- doing whatever I want. Often, especially when we are unreflective, we think of freedom in that simplistic way. When, as a teenager, I lived at home and my parents set hours when I had to be home, my "freedom" was limited. When I went away to college, I was "free" to stay out as late as I wished. There is of course a kernal of truth in this: the more extreme the extent of our limitation, the less free we are. Diplomats held hostage by terrorists, denied visitors and even exercise, are not free. But carried to its extreme, this view can suggest that freedom and limitation are inalterably opposed, that the ideal of true freedom would be that omnipotence in which we have no limits. It is this view which our play experience refutes. Let us remind ourselves, first, that nearly everyone associates play with freedom. We think first of spontaneous, relatively ungoverned play such as that of children; they are so free we think, and many of us try arbitrarily, sometimes desparately, to recapture that spontaneity. But even more rigorously structured play, such as organized games, even these we think of as places of freedom. We hurry from our average everyday activities down to the gym or tennis court, so that we may find that time of freedom, that "pause that refreshes". But is this not a paradox? We leave the relatively unstructured everyday world to enter a world of the most rigorous structure, the rule-governed domain of games; we submit ourselves therein to limitations both so strict and so arbitrary that we would never tolerate them in our ordinary lives if we did not choose them ourselves; and we do all this.... in order to be free! Despite appearances, it is not a paradox but an indication of the greater complexity of genuine freedom. For although it remains true that too much limitation inhibits freedom, it is also true that a certain modicum of finitude -- even if arbitrary as within games -- grants that realm, that de-fined world, wherein our freedom takes on a stake, an urgency, and so bestows its meaning. The limits of rules do give our actions in the game the meaning and urgency that is theirs. Forcing ourselves up against our limits of endurance and speed do reveal and indeed enhance our bodies' freedom. The boundaries and the time limits of a game perhaps most clearly of all do allow us to focus our consciousness and our bodies in such a way as to pursue to the end a set of possibilities, and so a realm of freedom.

The same connection between finitude and freedom is present in our everyday lives, though less visibly so. Why is the choice of a spouse under the more "limited" conditions of a single-spouse society so much more meaningful -- either positively or negatively -- than, for example, the "freer" choice of spouse number 190 out of an eventual 250? And if we were suddenly rendered immortal, would we, in joyful freedom from the restrictions of finitude, live our lives more fully and richly, or would we not rather lapse into an interminable boredom consequent upon the lack of urgency and a stake in our specific actions? Finitude gives us that urgency and stake; in choosing, freely choosing, within finitude, the choice for one act is a choice not for another. This fact, that every choosing is also always a "choosing not", that every affirmation is a negation, as Spinoza saw, is what gives our choices, and so our freedom, what meaning it has. Our play brings this home with special clarity because our play focuses itself, nourishes itself, on this situation and this recognition.

Earlier, I spoke of a teleological dimension to the issue of play. The considerations just discussed prepare us to take up that issue now, hopefully with greater clarity. The teleological issue arose insofar as the understanding of play as responsive openness began to suggest that this stance is a precarious achievement in which human beings become what they can be, fulfill themselves. To use the language of the ancient Greeks, in responsive openness, human beings achieve a kind of telos: end, goal, natural fulfillment. But the examples I then offered, pre-eminently those such as the pick-pocket or the mafia hit-man, render such a simple thesis problematic. Clearly, not all instances of responsive openness are those on which we would want to place a positive valuation. But as we have just reaffirmed, not all instances of responsive openness are play in any case. Could we then say either that all "good" instances of responsive openness are play, or at least that all play, or more fully, all playful instances of responsive openness are good? Unfortunately, no. That all good instances of responsive openness are not play is shown conclusively by examples such as guarding the president or controlling traffic safety at a large airport. No one, I take it, would regard such activities as play, yet they are paradigmatic of responsive openness. Nor is there strong plausibility in claiming that all play is good, or more fully, that all playful instances of responsive openness are good. For one thing, having characterized play in terms of responsive openness, even while recognizing that responsive openness is not <u>definitive</u> of play, to make the present claim we would be forced to seek some quality or qualities which distinguished "playful" from "unplayful" instances of responsive openness, an enterprise the cogency of which I have been arguing against. In any case, even if successful, we would be faced with considerable evidence that not even all generally accepted instances of play are good. What of those situations in which we say of someone that he or she is "just playing" with another person? What of the now notorious "games people play", or those situations in which we might scold someone, "Stop playing around and get to work!", or again, "You're just playing: get serious!"? What of those instances of play in which animosity breaks out among the players? When a person plays too roughly, is he or she not nevertheless playing? Finally, what of those apparent instances of play which we consider so risk-ful, or destructive, or trivial, as to be foolish: trying to drive automobiles across canyons, driving a large, gas-guzzling and polluting motor boat around a small lake when the world has an oil crisis, or fiddling while Rome burns?

Let us not concede the issue too hastily. The cases of "playing with people" and "games people play" can be parried by noting that with the characterization of play as a mode of responsive openness, these are not genuine instances of play. To "merely play with someone" is precisely not to be responsively open toward them; "games people play" are "roles" which we allow ourselves to assume, which again relieve us of the burden of being again and again responsively open to people in their individuality. Similarly, the standard oppositions of "play and work" as well as "play and seriousness" are undercut by understanding play as responsive openness. Most of us of course learn this experientially long before we can articulate and defend it. We are often most serious and work most hard just in our play. We can now see why. Responsive openness as a stance toward people and the world is so far from entailing non-seriousness and lack of work that it invites both high seriousness and work; these are false oppositions. Animosity or alienation, which sometimes occurs in play, is an aspect of the risk-full

70

character of much of our play to which I shall devote cosiderable attention subsequently. Here the point can be asserted simply; far from detracting from the value of play, risk-taking is part of its very appeal. The last two negative examples, the large motor boat polluting a lake and "fiddling while Rome burns" are examples not so much of the "badness" of play as a conflict between the value inherent in a given play experience and other values (environmental protection, the preserving of a city) which may conflict with or supercede them. So none of these seem to be cases where play is simply bad. Can we say, after all, that play is simply good?

We cannot, because the last two examples suggest the decisive point regarding the value of play. Although it may be true that we cannot think of examples of play which are inherently bad, we must nevertheless admit that there are situations and circumstances in which this or that instance of play, while remaining play, becomes bad. Is not the converse equally true? I doubt if we would have any more success coming up with an example of play which is intrinsically good. Our tendency to give play a positive valuation is rather based on the sense that in most of its instances it is affirmative and fulfilling. This in turn suggests how it stands with play. Play is neither noble or base "in itself". On the other hand, play is as far as possible from being "value free"[19] or "beyond good and evil". Our play is shot through with value, but the value present in it is not inherent. It has its source from elsewhere. The value of any given occasion of play is thus precarious; it can become either positive or negative. This is indeed part of the risk of play. Whence, then, does play derive its value?

Let us begin with the observation that not only all play but all instances of responsive openness, playful or unplayful, good or bad, are teleological. In every instance of responsive openness employed so far, responsive openness is itself a goal, even a demand, layed on the individual in question, however deplorable or honorable might be the task for which responsive openness is called. The mafia hit-man and the pick-pocket, the brain surgeon and the lion-tamer, the secret service agent and the air control officer, the skier and the basketball player, all are called upon to achieve responsive openness if they are to fulfill their projects. This is compatible with the

71

last point regarding the value of play. Whatever value we may place on a given activity on external grounds, responsive openness itself is a value to anyone who has accepted the project. Once I have accepted the project of killing the rival gang leader, or guarding the President, or performing a brain operation, or also skiing, playing basketball, fishing, or playing the guitar, responsive openness is a stance to be affirmed as valuable, to be sought and sustained. In this qualified sense, then, all play, indeed all responsive openness, is good. This may be the reason why we typically think of play as good altogether; we know that in our play we are called upon to achieve and sustain that stance wherein we are most alive and awake, responsive to our situation, in which we become what we truly can be.

The catch, of course, is that this or that project itself may carry a quite different value from the value inherent in the responsive openness exhibited within its horizon. Although I as a mafia hit-man may hold responsive openness a high value for the success of my project, few would hold the enterprise of murdering people in high regard. The same is true with any instance of play. The high value present for the skier in being responsively open to the snow and trails may be mitigated by our judgment that the skier, who happens to be an orthopedic surgeon, should have stopped his play to help the skier with the broken leg whom the surgeon nonchalantly passed by.

Hopefully we can now see and summarize something of the complexity of the issue of value in play. In one sense, play is inherently valuable; we recognize in the stance of responsive openness so characteristic of play a stance that is desirable whatever we do. But this "whatever we do" is subject to other standards and judgments of value, and on those occasions when the project itself is judged negatively, whether the project be playful or not, the positive value of the responsive openness therein is mitigated. In this sense we might say that play is valuable, but not the standard of value; it is a good, but it is not the Good.

One final point: one might observe that in this long chapter devoted to the stance of play, I have not even mentioned what, if anything, would be the definitive characteristic of play, fun. Might it not be said that it is just fun which distinguishes playful from non-playful instances of responsive openness? To be sure, killing people, or picking pockets, or guarding the president, or operating on people's brains, require responsive openness, but they are not -- usually -- considered play because they are not -- usually -- considered fun. Indeed, just insofar as an otherwise unplayful instance of responsive openness becomes fun, it begins to be play, as we witness with delight in that play about playful pick-pockets, "Oliver". This would also explain my earlier point that the distinction between play and non-play is not absolute but a matter of degree. Activities are more or less fun, and as a given activity becomes more and more fun, it becomes increasingly playful. Moreover, fun is also part at least of the value of play. We regard playful activities as carrying positive value because they are fun, and fun is a value, though, like responsive openness, not an unmitigated one. There are certain situations where having fun is inappropriate, where what is usually or "in itself" a good becomes, in certain contexts, a defect. The case of fun imitates that of responsive openness.

So it does, and it does so thoroughly enough that it too is not sufficient to "define" play. We enter the circle again: are all instances of play fun? Are all instances of fun play? The former claim is called into question by those numerous occasions when our play, intense, passionate, frustrating, hardly seems fun. It is hardly fun when we get injured in the heat of a physical contest, but was it any the less play at the time of injury? As for the latter case, it is sometimes "fun", especially when we are tired, to "do nothing", to "vegetate", say, in front of a television set. To be sure, for most of us that sort of fun is not long sustained; but it is, at the moment, fun, and it is neither responsive openness nor play.

Where do we stand with play? I have discussed several of what I regard as central elements in play: the stance of responsive openness, finitude, value, fun. Far from claiming that any of them are peculiar to play, however, I have tried to show how each of them are also present in our non-play experience, indeed, that part of the very value of play is that certain issues and themes present but often hidden in everyday life are highlighted in play and brought forth to the position of centrality which they should

73

perhaps have for us always. What about all of them together? Do these four themes combined constitute a definition of play, such that their convergence occurs in all play and in nothing but play? In no way. I am sure that the refutation of that view awaits only the next imaginative example. Nor would I wish to claim that these four elements exhaust the qualities, even the important qualities, of play. But they do strike me as central and worthy of reflection. To repeat, then, and close this section: my goal has been to reflect upon and deepen our appreciation of certain themes central to, but not exclusive to, play. That effort will continue in Section III. The point of philosophic reflection of this sort is to seek clarification, not definition. We seek opening, not closure.

Footnotes, Chapter 4

1). An earlier and much shorter version of this chapter was given as the Presidential Address of the Philosophic Society for the Study of Sport at its 8th Annual Meeting in Karlsruhe, West Germany, July 7, 1980, and subsequently published in the Journal of the Philosophy of Sport, Volume VII, 1980, under the title, "The Stance of Play".

2). There is an excellent, but unfortunately unpublished paper on this topic -- what amounts to a phenomenology of skiing -- entitled "Dust of Snow", by a former student of mine, James Wolcott.

3). Compare Suits, Bernard, The Grasshopper: Games, Life, Utopia, Toronto, University of Toronto Press, 1978, with McBride, Frank, "Toward a Non-Definition of Sport", Journal of the Philosophy of Sport, Volume II, 1975, pp. 4-11.

4). I shall retain both the phrases, "human nature" and human being". "Human nature" carries with it the notion of endurance through time, if not of permanence, and "human being" brings out, through its verbal structure, the sense of activity and process. I want to retain both senses.

5). For a longer discussion of this issue, see Plato, Charmides 166d, and my book, The Virtue of Philosophy: An Interpretation of Plato's Charmides, Athens, Ohio, Ohio University Press, 1981.

6). Kierkegaard, Soren, The Journals of Kierkegaard, edited by Alexander Dru, New York, Harper and Row, 1958, page 134. See also pages 116, 117, 121, 133-135. Philosophical Fragments, translated by David Swenson, Princeton, Princeton University Press, 1936, pages 14, 28, 128; Concluding Unscientific Postscript, translated by David Swenson, Princeton, Princeton University Press, 1941, pages 20, 128, 138, 217, 219.

7). Nietzsche, Friedrich, Thus Spoke Zarathustra, in The Portable Nietzsche, edited by Walter Kaufmann, New York, Viking Press, 1954, pages 304-304.

8). A good example of the appeal of this position is the popularity of Kahlil Gibran's books, especially The Prophet, New York, Knopf, 1966.

9). Marx, Karl, On the Jewish Question in Karl Marx: Early Writings, translated and edited by T.B. Bottomore, New York, McGraw-Hill, 1963, page 25, 26.

10). Marx, Karl, "Theses on Feuerbach", in The German Ideology, edited by C.J. Arthur, New York, International Publishers, 1970, page 122.

11). Buber, Martin, I And Thou, New York, Charles Scribner's Sons, 1958, page 4.

12). Kant, Immanuel, Idea for a Universal History with a Cosmopolitan Intent, in The Philosophy of Kant, edited by Carl Friedrick, New York, The Modern Library, 1949, page 120.

13). See, for example, the entire prologue to Thus Spoke Zarathustra.

14). E.G. Galileo, Opere Complete di Galileo Galilei (Firenze, 1842), IV, 171. Descartes, Meditationes de Prima Philosophia, Paris, Librairie Philosophique de J. Vrin, 1960, Meditation II, Pages 24, 25. Machiavelli, The Prince and Other Discourses, New York, Modern Library, 1950, see especially page 94. Bacon, Instauratio Magnus, Preface. See also Novum Organum, Aphorism CXXIX: "But if a man endeavors to establish and extend the power and dominion of the human race itself over the universe, his ambition....is without doubt a more wholesome thing and more noble than the other two." Kant, Critique of Pure Reason, translated by Norman Kemp Smith, London, McMillan & Co., 1961, page 20, G.B. Vico, On the Most Ancient Wisdom of the Italians, Part II "On the Origin and Truth of the Sciences".

15). Hegel, G.F.W., The Phenomenology of Spirit, translated by A.V. Miller, Oxford, Clarendon Press, 1977, page 111-119.

16). Suits, op.cit. pages 24 ff. et al.

17). Ibid, page 60 ff.

18). For an extended discussion of this issue see Morgan, Wm., "Play, Utopia and Dystopia: Prologue to a Ludic Theory of the State", unpublished.

19). C.F. Hans, James S., The Play of the World, Amherst, University of Massachusetts Press, 1981, page 130. I shall have further occasion to comment on this stimulating book in the following chapter.

PART III

Chapter 5: Play Decentered: An Alternative

For the most part, the balance of this book will be concerned with the development of some of the consequences of my conception of play. But before doing so, I wish to consider and respond to what I consider the most important contemporary alternative to the conception of play just developed. The fundamental standpoint of this alternative is quite familiar; its guiding paradigm is child's play, with its connotations of spontaneity, freedom, whimsicality, purposelessness, unpredictability, and irrationality.

This understanding of play is manifest in our culture generally. It is sometimes praised as a source and sign of freedom, spontaneity, and exhuberance, yet at other times denigrated as indicating a lack of seriousness, a frivolousness about life, or a refusal to "grow up". For my purposes, however, its most interesting and challenging presence occurs in an area of contemporary philosophy itself; I refer to the philosophical movement in Europe sometimes loosely called "continental philosophy", whose representatives include Nietzsche, Heidegger, Gadamer, Eugen Fink, Jacques Derrida, and Michael Foucault. For all these thinkers, as I shall presently show, this conception of play modeled after child's play plays an important role, not always as an explicit theme for investigation but as a guiding metaphor for some decisive aspect of their philosophy, whether it be the will to power, Being, history, language, or interpretation.

I hope in this chapter to establish a number of points. First, I want to acknowledge that this conception of play is an important alternative to my own. Second and related to this, I want to show that such an understanding of play is revealing, but also concealing, that it both exhibits important possibilities for human being and for our understanding of the world, yet is limited in such a way as to be at best a partial account. Third, I want to show that and how this conception of play as whimsical and irrational is shared by the thinkers mentioned above as a guiding metaphor for some important aspect of their thought, and so that the limitations of this conception of play will constitute a limitation on their positions. Finally, I wish to show that and how there is an intimate connection between their understanding of play and their conception of the individual, just as in the last chapter I showed how my own conception of play is grounded in an understanding of the individual as both monadic and relational, incomplete yet overfull, and vacillating between the stances of dominance and submission.

To repeat, the conception of play at work here is easy to state succinctly and relatively free of conceptual difficulties. First, play is irrational (it is important to remember that this characteristic is rarely meant pejoratively by the spokesmen for this view. It is usually simply descriptive, and sometimes appears to be almost a term of approbation). Recall Huizinga's succinct development of this point discussed in Chapter 3. Play, Huizinga tells us, "resists all analysis, all logical interpretation,"[1] it "cannot have its foundations in any rational nexus,"[2] and so, "play is irrational."[3] What is it about play, more precisely, that leads to its characterization as irrational? I suspect there are two primary factors involved. The first, alluded to by Huizinga's reference to its lack of a "rational nexus", is its apparent resistance to or independence from causal explanation. What is often called the spontaneity of play probably refers to this fact, that we do not experience our play as "caused" by previous events, either physical or psychical. The play impulse seems rather to "burst forth" from time to time, sporadically, without planning, without cause. As Heidegger puts it, play is "without why".[4] Second, just as, in this sense, play is without an arche, so it is also often experienced as without a telos. We are told that play is "purposeless", that it has no end beyond itself, and so, to use a term of approbation, that it is "autotelic".[5] It is easy to see the extent to which the play of children rather than, say, the play of the gifted athlete, is the paradigm for this conception of play.[6]

Several initial observations should be made about this. Note, first, that this supposed irrational element can be and usually is asserted in positive terms as one of the virtues of play. Play on this view is spontaneous and free (i.e. uncaused); it is an end unto itself, not a mere means to other ends (i.e. it is autotelic). As such, to sum up in a now well-known phrase, it is "an oasis of happiness....in the desert of our questing".[7] But it must be observed that from another standpoint, or perhaps in another mood, these same characteristics can be viewed negatively. Play, as irrational, is frivolous, non-serious, unpredictable and so undependable. More deeply, as without either <u>arche</u> (ground) or <u>telos</u> (purpose), it is an abyss <u>(Ab-grund)</u>. We shall appreciate the significance of this more fully as we turn to the modern figures whose philosophies are informed by this understanding of play.

A second observation: while this conception of play is plausible enough for certain sorts of play -- again the paradigm of child's play comes to mind -- it is clear that it is hardly sufficient as a comprehensive account of play. Most if not all sports, to take the most obvious counter-example, are both <u>arche</u>-ological and <u>tele</u>-ological (in both the auto-telic and "hetero-telic" senses of the term), as are such diverse play activities as playing games (chess, checkers), playing a musical instrument, or playing a part in a play.[8] Part of my own intention in developing my characterization of play as responsive openness was to articulate a stance true of most instances of play, and so not dependent on one paradigm or another. We shall consider in greater detail the significance of play paradigms when we turn to Nietzsche. Here I wish simply to establish that the interpretation of play as irrational is radically partial, at best appropriate for only one mode of play, and a limited mode at that.

A third observation: even if we operate within the paradigm of child's play, is it uncontroversial that play is uncaused and without <u>telos</u>? Under what conception of cause is play without cause, "without why"? In any case, is to be without cause equivalent to being without <u>arche</u>, without ground? The point is, if one element in the supposed irrationality of play is its lack of cause, then we had better be clear and precise about the sense of cause at work here. To take only one famous example, suppose we apply the Aristotelian teaching regarding the "four causes" to play; would play be uncaused, or would it not rather have its own proper mode of causality, and in this sense be altogether rational? To say the least, the claim that play is without cause hides a host of ambiguities. The same is true of the supposed non-teleological character of play. Is to say that

81

play is autotelic to deny teleology or not rather precisely to assert the specific mode of teleology that belongs to it?

Finally, even if we grant that in some sufficiently qualified sense, such play is without cause and without purpose, does that make it irrational? Or are we not thereby under the sway of an all too narrow and inadequate interpretation of rationality? With such questions in mind, let us turn to a consideration of the penetrating way in which this understanding of play is employed by the previously cited modern thinkers. We begin with Nietzsche.

The appeal of a conception of play as child's play to Nietzsche can be seen first in his very early work, Philosophy In the Tragic Age of the Greeks, in his appreciation of Heraclitus. Heraclitus, the great Pre-Socratic spokesman for becoming and flux as fundamental in the cosmos, appeals strongly to all the thinkers to be discussed here, and especially appealing in this regard is his famous fragment 52 (D-K) which reads as follows: "Time (or lifetime: aion) is a child playing, playing at draughts. Kingship belongs to a child."[9] I hope it is not scholarly knit-picking to note, first, that Nietzsche -- and following him, Heidegger, Gadamer, Fink, Foucault, and Derrida -- interprets this fragment in a somewhat extreme way, emphasizing the notion of a "child playing" (pais paizon) and subordinating or even neglecting the fact that Heraclitus' metaphor portrays the child playing at draughts, a game with rules and ordered moves. Neglecting this and concentrating on the "child playing", Nietzsche is able to establish the image of play that appeals to him:

> "In this world only play, play as artists
> and children engage in it, exhibits coming
> to be and passing away, structuring and
> destroying, without any moral additive, in
> forever equal innocence. And as children
> and artists play, so plays the everliving
> fire. It constructs and destroys, all in
> innocence. Such is the game that the aeon
> plays with itself."[10]

It is important to see at the outset how crucial the paradigm of child's play is here. Suppose, for example, that Nietzsche had chosen instead the image of the gifted athlete, a favorite paradigm of play for the Greeks.[11] Then presumably, themes such as competition, training, skill, gracefulness, tolerance of pain, "the thrill of victory and the agony of defeat" would have emerged as the dominant ones. I say this to emphasize once again that Nietzsche's paradigm, though it may -- controversially -- be a paradigm for one mode of play, in no way constitutes a general model for any and all play.

This image of play as childlike, amoral, innocent, spontaneous, whimsical, creative yet (as all creation is for Nietzsche) destructive, is sustained in Nietzsche's mature work as an image both for the most noble kind of life and for the way in which the will to power manifests itself as the coursing of the world. No better text for this can be found than Thus Spoke Zarathustra. The hero of that philosophical novel, Zarathustra, is himself characterized as a child and a dancer.[12] Moreover, in a decisive section of the book, "The Three Metamorphoses," Zarathustra teaches that one must first be a camel, then become a lion, but finally become a child, who "is innocence and forgetting, a new beginning, a game, a self-propelled wheel, a first movement, a sacred 'Yes'."[13] Later we are told that "A real man wants two things: danger and play."[14] In the section entitled "The Stillest Hour," where Zarathustra is still too afraid of affirming the eternal recurrence of the same, the voice tells him that he "must yet become as a child and without shame."[15] It is important to see that in becoming like a child and playful in this sense, Zarathustra is simply getting into an attunement with the way the world happens as will to power. He informs us that he "would only believe in a god who could dance,"[16] and speaking of the belief in permanence and unity he says,

> "Evil I call it, and misanthropic -- all
> this teaching of the One and the Plenum
> and the Unmoved and the Sated and the
> Permanent. All the permanent, that is
> only a parable. And the poets lie too
> much. It is of time and becoming that
> the best parables speak: let them be a
> praise and a justification of all
> impermanence."[17]

83

Decisively, in Part III, in a section entitled "Before Sunrise", Zarathustra reiterates this teaching in such a way that his understanding of the world-happening is unmistakable:

> "Verily, it is a blessing and not a blasphemy when I teach: ´Over all things stand the heaven Accident, the heaven Innocence, the heaven Chance, the heaven Prankishness.´ ´By chance´ -- that is the most ancient nobility of the world, and this I restored to all things: I delivered them from their bondage under Purpose. This freedom and heavenly cheer I have placed over all things like an azure bell when I taught that over them and through them no ´eternal will´ wills. This prankish folly I have put in the place of that will when I taught: ´In everything one thing is impossible: rationality.´"[18]

To sum up what I hope is now obvious: Nietzsche is guided both in his conception of the best life ("real men") and his understanding of the happening of things, by the metaphor of child´s play, where that metaphor is taken to imply spontaneity, purposelessness, chance, amorality, irrationality, and his peculiar notion of innocent yet destructive creativity. As we shall see, the other thinkers to be considered take this image almost unaltered and apply it to equally fundamental aspects of their own thought. Let us turn next to Heidegger.

Regarding the theme of play in Heidegger´s thinking, two points need to be established. First, Heidegger sustains the model of play present in Nietzsche as irrational child´s play. Second, he employs this metaphor as a guiding image for the play of Being or the happening of things, and especially for the play of Being with human being (Dasein).[19]

The best locus for Heidegger´s understanding both of play itself and of the play of Being is his as yet untranslated work, Der Satz vom Grund.[20] In that work, Heidegger reflects on the Leibnizian "Principle of Ground" or "Principle of Reason" as the culmination of the standpoint of metaphysics. In an effort to overcome that standpoint, which assumes that everything, including Being itself, has a "ground" or "reason", Heidegger appeals to the notion of play. But, he warns, we must not take play in its usual sense, where it is construed as a thing which, like any-thing else, must be "grounded" or "justified" by something else.[21] Rather, play is a ´mystery´,[22] to be understood precisely as ground-less, as Ab-grund (the German word usually translated as "abyss"). Citing Heraclitus´ fragment 52 on the aion, he comments, "Das Seinsgeschick: ein Kind, das spielt" (The happening of Being: a child who plays)[23], and adds,

> "It plays because it plays. ´Because´
> sinks away in play. The play is without
> ´why´. It plays for the while that it
> plays. There remains only play: the
> highest and deepest."[24]

So far, it is easy enough to see the kinship between Heidegger´s understanding of play and that of Nietzsche developed earlier. We saw that Nietzsche applied his conception of play both as a description of the way the world, as will to power, "happens", and as a recommendation to the "higher men" as the best stance to take as a response to that happening. The case is similar with Heidegger. The play which happens like a child´s play, without why, is the play of Being. As the passage from Der Satz vom Grund quoted above makes clear, it is das Seinsgeschick, the "happening," "destiny," or "mission" of Being, which is a child playing. Moreover, the play of Being is a playing with human being. Alternatively, given the affinity of language and Being for Heidegger, language plays with human being, not vice-versa:

> "If we may talk here of playing games at
> all, it is not we who play with words, but
> the nature of language plays with us, not
> only now, but long since and always. For
> language plays with our speech -- it likes
> to let our speech drift away into the more
> obvious meaning of words."[25]

Moreover, it should be understood that this play of Being/language with human being is nothing friendly or amusing, but deadly serious:

> "This floundering in commonness is part
> of the high and dangerous game and gamble
> in which, by the nature of language, we
> are the stakes."[26]

John Caputo is thus accurate when he describes the
play of Being as a "fearful play,"[27] as "deadly
serious,"[28] and adds elsewhere that "Being as play
is wanton and unpredictable."[29] Thus what Nietzsche
characterized as the destructive element in the
innocent creativity of play is preserved by Heidegger
in the ominous sense in which Being "plays with" human
being. At the slight risk of exaggeration, we might
say that this is less the "playing with" of friends
than the "playing with" of a captured mouse by a cat.

There is at least one more important similarity
between the understanding of play in Nietzsche and
Heidegger. We saw that for Nietzsche, play was the
proper stance to be taken by the "higher men" toward
the happening of things. Thus play, in the sense he
developed, was recommended as the best way to be. In
less straightforwardly hortatory terms, Heidegger says
the same thing. The last line of Der Satz vom Grund
reads:

> "The question remains whether and how we,
> hearing the movements of this playing, play
> along with and join in the playing."[30]

Perhaps we might sum up this discussion by taking
note of perhaps the strongest difference between the
Heideggerian and Nietzschean understandings of play, a
difference hinted at, perhaps, by Heidegger's apparent
reluctance straightforwardly to recommend play as a
stance for human being. However much they may agree
both on the nature of play as irrational (to use a
covering term for this conception) and on the role of
play both in the world and for human being, Heidegger
seems more impressed by the ominous, dangerous,
destructive character of the play of Being; at least,
he is more sobered by it, less enthusiastic about
"saying yes" to it than Nietzsche. One might say that
whereas Nietzsche urges us exhuberantly to affirm this
dangerous play, Heidegger somberly intones that we
should take a stance of releasement (Gelassenheit)
toward it. To say the least, Nietzsche's is the more
playful stance toward the play of Being.

Finally, we must ask what will be the direction of the play of human being for Heidegger, insofar as we do "play along with and join in the playing." As Der Satz vom Grund makes clear, it means at least a giving up of the "Principle of Ground," the effort to understand, explain, and justify everything on a rational basis. But this, on Heidegger's view, is tantamount to a giving up of metaphysics or even philosophy, which is why Heidegger claims just this throughout his later work. Caputo puts the point succinctly: "Dasein must give up philosophy and metaphysics altogether in order to 'play along with' (mitspielen) the play of Being."[31] I hope to show in detail in my last chapter that and how this standpoint represents a radical misinterpretation of the nature both of play and of philosophy. Here I can close with the reiteration of an observation made earlier regarding Nietzsche: the paradigm of child's play after which this view is modeled is at most one among several modes of play. It therefore cannot be comprehensive nor, consequently, should our view of the world be founded upon it. Once again, however, this is not to deny its efficacy within a certain sphere. We can appreciate more of this efficacy by a consideration of the role of play in the thought of Hans-Georg Gadamer.

It is curious that although both the thinkers so far considered insist on the purposeless or -- in tension with that -- autotelic character of play, both use play for a telos other than itself: as a metaphor for the happening of the world and for human comportment. The same is true for the role of play in the thought of Gadamer. He too does not treat play as a matter for thought in its own right. Instead, his most extended discussion of play occurs early in his magnum opus, Truth and Method, where he discusses the nature of play as a path into an appreciation of aesthetic experience, which in turn is to be employed to open up the issue of truth in the human sciences, the topic with which the work is centrally concerned. Nevertheless, certain aspects of his understanding of play are especially challenging to the conception of play I espouse.

As is well-known, Gadamer is deeply influenced by Heidegger. Not surprisingly, then, his fundamental conception of play begins with the Nietzschean/Heideggerian standpoint which we have already considered. For Gadamer too, the guiding

87

metaphor for play is child's play, although he tries
to develop this into its "perfection" in art.[32] He
regularly appeals explicitly to child's play as the
paradigm,[33] and his specific examples of play
situations are typically children's games ("tinker,
tailor, soldier sailor," children playing motor cars,
children dressing up).[34] Like Nietzsche and
Heidegger, he insists that central to play is that it
is "without goal or purpose,"[35] it has "no goal
which brings it to an end,"[36] yet -- again in
tension with this -- that it is autotelic:

> "The being of all play is always
> realization, sheer fulfillment,
> energeia, which has its telos within
> itself."[37]

However, from this fundamental understanding
common to Nietzsche and Heidegger, Gadamer emphasizes
different dimensions of the play experience in such a
way as to constitute a penetrating challenge to my own
view. To be specific, I entitled Part II, in which I
developed the foundation of my own understanding of
play, "The Stance of Play". In so doing, I emphasized
what I subsequently called the "intentional" character
of play, that it has to do most fundamentally with the
stance, mode of comportment, or attitude of the
player. It is precisely this which Gadamer denies.
Perhaps taking his cue from the Heideggerian point
that the essential play is the play of Being with
human being, Gadamer insists that play is not to be
located at all in the consciousness of the player, but
that play simply "happens" to the player independently
of his or her intentions. His position can be
succinctly stated by a judicious selection of quotes:

> "We can certainly distinguish between
> play and the attitude of the player,
> which, as such, belongs with the other
> attitudes of subjectivity."[38]

> "Play fulfills its purpose only if the
> player loses himself in his play."[39]

> "Our question concerning the nature of
> play itself cannot, therefore, find an
> answer if we look to the subjective
> reflection of the player to provide it.
> Instead, we are enquiring into the mode

of being of play as such."[40]

"For play has its own essence, independent of the consciousness of those who play."[41]

"The players are not the subjects of play; instead play merely reaches presentation through the players."[42]

"It is the game that is played -- it is irrelevant whether or not there is a subject who plays."[43]

"Hence the mode of being of play is not such that there must be a subject who takes up a playing attitude in order that the game may be played."[44]

This notion, along with Heidegger's notion of the play of Being, will be seen presently to be an important source for Eugen Fink's important conception of "play without a player". But we shall take that position up in detail presently. Here, I want to begin by acknowledging at least the partial phenomenological plausibility of Gadamer's view. It seems true enough that sometimes at least, a particular situation becomes playful even though none of the participants began with the intention to make it so. Moreover, Gadamer's view can make some sense of the occasional episode where a number of participants in an acitivity might intend to be playful, but in spite of their good intentions the activity never attains to genuine playfulness. It is easy to see how, putting these two possibilities together, it is tempting to infer, with Gadamer, that the attitude of the player has nothing to do with whether or not there is play. Nevertheless, I believe that it is a faulty inference.

It is true enough that sometimes we intend to be playful but fail. I never said that the stance of play -- responsive openness -- was easy; to the contrary, I argued explicitly that it is a difficult and precarious achievement, subject always to a collapse into its poles of dominance or submission. Similarly, it is true that often a situation becomes playful independently of the explicit intention of one or all of the participants. Again, I never suggested that the stance of responsive openness only occurs

89

when someone self-consciously intends it as a project.
To the contrary. What I do insist is that whenever
there is play, there is also the stance of responsive
openness by the players, whether or not it was their
original intention. I add that the possibility of
play happening is enhanced -- but not guaranteed --
when the putative players take on the project of being
responsively open. In this way, my own view can
account for the cases Gadamer's view raises, and
nothing in his view leads me, finally, to abandon my
position. This is not to say, of course, that his
view is not penetrating and insightful.

There is, however, one consequence of Gadamer's
specific position which I would hold is
phenomenologically false, and I should at least point
this out before moving on to Fink's notion of play.
Gadamer himself virtually acknowledges this
consequence:

> "Play itself is, rather, transformation
> of such a kind that the identity of the
> player does not continue to exist for
> anybody."[45]

That would indeed seem consistent with his view that
play is radically independent of the player. But if
so, would it not follow, especially when this is
coupled with the insistence that "Play fulfills its
purpose only if the player loses himself in his
play,"[46] that there is no self-knowledge possible or
available in play? To say the least, if I "lose
myself," if my "identity....does not continue to exist
for anybody," it is difficult to see what
self-knowledge would possibly mean in this context.
Yet all the disciplines I discussed in Part I, but
especially psychology, insisted with great
plausibility that the play situation is a rich theatre
for self-knowledge, and I tried to sustain that claim
in Part II by showing how the stance of play is indeed
grounded in a certain conception of the self, which
can therefore be known in and through play. As we
shall see later in this chapter when we turn to the
conception of the self held by these thinkers, there
is a reason why they would hold that play is not a
source of self-knowledge. Here I close with the
observation that the claim that self-knowledge is not
available in play is phenomenologically false, as I
have shown in Parts I and II. Any conception of play,

therefore, which implies such an impossibility is thereby highly questionable.

None of the thinkers discussed so far have treated play thematically, in its own right. Of the six thinkers we are to consider in this chapter, Eugen Fink is the only one to do so in a sustained way. He has written a book on play, <u>Spiel als Weltsymbol</u> ("Play as World-symbol"),[47] as well as a shorter monograph with the attractive title, <u>Oase des Glucks: Gedanken zu einer Ontologie des Spiels</u>("Oasis of Happiness: Thoughts on an Ontology of Play")[48]. What we find in these works, however, is for the most part a more detailed, more thorough setting out of the general conception of play held by the previously discussed thinkers. To be sure, Fink develops this conception with some interesting and somewhat different emphases, to which I shall subsequently turn. First, however, it is important to show that the general view of play espoused is the now familiar one modeled after child's play.

Both <u>Spiel als Weltsymbol</u> and "The Ontology of Play" regularly appeal to child's play as the paradigm of play. At one point in "The Ontology of Play", Fink seems to qualify this paradigm in an important way:

> "Everything considered, perhaps we would not want to say that ideal play is that of the child. The adult can also play, but in a different way that is more furtive, more masked. If we take our notion of play from the world of the child alone, we misunderstand its nature, fall into equivocation. In fact, the domain of play extends from the little girl's playing with a doll to the tragedy."[49]

One wishes that Fink had sustained this qualification in greater depth, which might have led him not to model his understanding of play so exclusively after child's play. Unfortunately, he does not; more true to his actual understanding of play is the last line of "The Ontology of Play," which concludes:

> "When philosophers and poets stress the power and meaning of play as a profound human reality, perhaps we should remember

the words that warn us that we will not
enter into the kingdom of heaven unless
we become like little children."[50]

Not surprisingly, given this paradigm, Fink
associates with play many of the same attributes we
have seen before. Play is purposeless, goalless.[51]
Indeed, it "stands out in remarkable relief to all
that characterizes life teleologically."[52]
Similarly, it is groundless; Fink emphasizes that it
is in play that there appears the groundlessness,
goallessness, even the worthlessness of things, of
world.[53] On the other hand, and again in keeping
with the tension we have observed previously, play,
though non-teleological, is nevertheless autotelic; it
has a _telos_, within itself.[54] Nevertheless, as
without ground or _telos_, play takes on the sense in
Fink too of being irrational; for him, it is literally
thought-less:

> "Der spielende Mensch denkt nicht und
> der denkende Mensch spielt nicht."
> ("The playing man does not think and the
> thinking man does not play").[55]

Again, play is spontaneous and free.[56]

Decisively, Fink also sees in play not just a
human phenomenon but a metaphor or "symbol" for the
world (a "World-symbol"). He joins the other thinkers
discussed in citing Heraclitus´ fragment 52 ("Time is
a child playing, playing draughts. Kingship is in the
hands of the child"), as his favorite _locus classicus_
for this view, once again failing to take account of
the fact that time in the Heraclitean fragment is
presented as playing a rule-governed game.[57] Human
play is thus a symbol for world-play, as the title of
his main book on play suggests, and that world-play is
consequently to be understood as the purposeless,
non-teleological, unpredictable, irrational, and
spontaneous happening of things.[58] Fink explicitly
congratulates Nietzsche for this insight:

> "Where Nietzsche grasps Being and
> Becoming as play, he no longer stands
> in the confinement of metaphysics."[59]

This means, specifically, that for Fink too, the decisive significance of play is not human play but that world-play which is the play of Being with human being.[60] The unpredictable, groundless and goalless happening of Being is thus "play without a player."[61]

So far, Fink´s understanding of play has been shown to be essentially similar to that of the other thinkers cited, and I would want to make the same observations about it, recognizing on the one hand its insightfulness as a characterization of one mode of play, but also questioning the exclusivity of the paradigm of child´s play and subsequently the implications regarding the supposed irrationality of play. I now wish to turn to several important nuances to Fink´s view which should be emphasized.

First, although to be sure Fink transfers his notion of human play to play as world-symbol, he does not follow Gadamer in denying to play its "subjective" element. In other words, the world may indeed be "play without a player", but Fink at least holds that for human play there are indeed players, and their "subjective state" is integral to what human play is.

> "We can indicate at first sight, as an essential element of play, that it is a passion of the soul. We can say that all man is and does is colored by either one or the other states of the soul -- joy, sadness, or the gray tone of indifference. Play, at least in its source, has the coloring of joy."[62]

On the one hand, this means that Fink can preserve (with me) the insistence that at least in the realm of human play there is an intimate connection between play and the stance of the player. On the other hand, he runs the risk of losing the sense of symmetry between the spheres of "human play" and "Being-play" that Gadamer was able to maintain by insisting that even in the human realm the consciousness of the player was insignificant. For Fink, it becomes somewhat awkward to insist that "an essential element of play (is) that it is a passion of the soul",[63] yet characterize the world or Being as "play without a player".

Second, Fink sustains a reflection on another controversial aspect of play largely ignored by the previous thinkers: the question of the "reality" of play. The issue is a familiar one. Often the play "world" is explicitly contrasted to the "real" world (which in these contexts usually refers to the "work" world -- a noteworthy prejudice). Play is often referred to as an "escape" from the "real" world, a pause that refreshes us so that we can return to the "serious business of life" invigorated. When to this is added the presence in much of our play of creative imagination and in some cases make-believe (again, the paradigm of child's play comes first to mind), it is easy to see how play becomes contrasted to our everyday experience as unreality to reality. Yet on the other hand, the depth of our immersion in our experience of play, the passion and energy we invest in it, as well as the insight into ourselves, our fellow humans, and the world available in it, argue if anything for the heightened "reality" of play. Fink sees both sides of the issue and holds them together in a thoughtful balance. On the one hand, he acknowledges, play does seem to have about it a different structure from "reality": "The dominant and compelling accents in the rhythm of human life do not occur in play."[64] On the other hand, Fink sees immediately that play is not something unreal but "a curious mixture of ´Being´ and ´Semblance´,"[65] and he develops this ambivalence at considerable length.[66] He puts the issue well in "The Ontology of Play":

> "We play in the world which we call
> real, but in so doing, we create for
> ourselves another world, a mysterious
> one. This is not just nothing and
> still it is not something real either.
> In the world of play we act according
> to our role; but in this world imaginary
> persons live, as the ´child´ which takes
> on body and life, but which is nothing
> more than a doll or even a piece of wood
> in reality."[67]

I note in passing the clear continuation of the paradigm of child's play. The "unreality" here derives primarily from the creative imaginativeness characteristic of certain modes of play. This characteristic, it should be noted, is considerably less forceful if one thinks not so much of child's play but of, say, a soccer game. Whence, then, for Fink, comes the reality of play? Interestingly enough, its reality derives from the knowledge available in the play world of the "real world", indeed of the "essences" of all things":[68]

> "Human play (even if we no longer
> recognize it as such after a while)
> is the symbolic action which puts us
> in the presence of the meaning of the
> world and of life."[69]

It is as if the very "unreality" of that "oasis of happiness" which is the play-world offers us the "distance" necessary genuinely to understand our everyday world. One is reminded here of the etymological connection in Greek between "play" (paidia) and "education" (paideia) as well as the famous remark of Albert Camus that only in sports did he ever learn anything about ethics.[70]

About this curious co-presence of reality and unreality in play as Fink understands it I wish to make several observations. The first I have already touched upon. The notion of play as having a component of unreality has its strongest force when the paradigm of play is taken to be the make-believe play of children -- playing house, playing with dolls, etc. The further one gets from that paradigm, for instance if one takes a a model of play a competitive sport such as soccer, or the pastime of fishing, or even having a catch, the less significant the component of unreality becomes. One is forced to appeal then to the fact that the "stakes" are typically not so dramatic in games as in "real life," although if one takes account of the depth of psychological investment some of us make in our play, even this is dubious.

This leads to a second observation. It may be that the element of "unreality" in play only has a strong sense in a specific and limited mode of play, and that it is wrong, therefore, to take it as a decisive or "essential" aspect of play. In short, for many of us, our play is every bit as "real" (a word that, after all, would need elaborate clarification and qualification) as anything else we do.

However, this in no way mitigates the other point that Fink ties to the reality/unreality issue, namely, that the play-world is a potential source of deep insight into ourselves and our world. I have strongly agreed with this point in the development of my own conception of play in Part II, and that claim is in no way mitigated by my contention that in addition to being insightful most of our play is also very real. Contrary to the implication of Fink, then, the revelatory power of play is utterly independent of its supposed "unreality".

I close the discussion of Fink's notion of play with a final observation. Large sections of Fink's major work on play, Spiel als Weltsymbol, are not explicitly about play but about Plato; Fink offers a sustained criticism of what he regards as the unplayful character of Platonic philosophy and the culture (the west) and metaphysics (western metaphysics) that is founded on it. His general point seems to be that Plato does not so much overlook play as denigrate it to the realm of "mere appearance" and so dismisses it from the realm of the "essence of things".[71] Since this is a book on play and not on Fink's interpretation of Plato, I shall not embark on a elaboration of his Plato interpretation, which I consider deeply erroneous. But in my last chapter, I shall develop my own understanding of the relation of play to philosophy which will have a strong "Platonic" component. That chapter may fairly be taken as an implied reply to Fink's interpretation of Plato's teaching on play.

I turn now to two contemporary French thinkers whose influence is now beginning to be felt world-wide, not just in professional philosophy but in literature, art, and history as well: Jacques Derrida and Michel Foucault. I remind the reader that my point in considering this large number of modern thinkers is to give some sense of just how pervasive a certain conception of play is. Since the details of the conception of play and how it is employed have now been developed at some length, I shall move somewhat more quickly through these last two cases.

In brief, Derrida too adopts the conception of play as child's play, once again derived from Nietzsche. Indeed, in L'ecriture et la Difference, developing this theme of the play of things, he makes this derivation explicit, writing of

"....the Nietzschean affirmation, the
joyous affirmation, of the play of the
world and of the innocence of becoming,
the affirmation of a world of signs
without fault, without truth, without
origin, offered to an active interpretation..."[72]

Once again we see implied the same understanding
of play as groundless, whimsical, irrational in the
sense discussed. What is of special interest in
Derrida is the field to which he applies play as a
metaphor: language and knowledge. The pursuit of
knowledge, which for many of us has as its paradigm
science, with its deep concern with rigorous,
systematic, even mathematical methodology, is, as
Derrida sees it, not this at all, but play:

"Knowledge is not a systematic tracking
down of a truth that is hidden but may
be found. It is rather the field of
freeplay, that is to say, a field
of infinite substitutions in the closure
of a finite ensemble."[73]

But the primary application of the metaphor of
play for Derrida is language itself. The "play of
language",[74] the "play of signifying references
which constitute language,"[75] refers to Derrida's
convictions regarding the "decentered" character of
words and language. Words have no meaning "in
themselves;" they are in this sense groundless, but
take on what meaning they have only in terms of the
surrounding words, context, even epoch, which itself
is not grounded but "flowing" freely. Thus he insists
in Of Grammatology that,

"The study of the functioning of language,
of its play, presupposes that the
substance of meaning, and among other
possible substances, that of sound, be
placed in parenthesis."[76]

The old-fashioned notion, then, that words have
"intrinsic" or even "established" meanings which
ground their use, and in the light of which a given
use of a word can be judged correct or incorrect,

rational or irrational, has been shown, according to Derrida, to be itself groundless and irrational. The accurate understanding of the "happening" of language is, again, as irrational, free-flowing (that is, without logic), play.

Finally, Derrida, like several of the thinkers previously cited, places special significance on this metaphor of play because it symbolizes for him the overcoming of the "logocentrism", the emphasis on and assumption of logic and causal order in the happening of things, which has characterized western culture or "metaphysics". Thus,

> "One could call play the absence
> of the transcendental signified as
> limitlessness of play, that is to say,
> as the destruction of onto-theology
> and the metaphysics of presence."[77]

To summarize and move on to Foucault: for Derrida, play, and especially the play of language, refers to its "happening" which is without ground or cause and without purpose, which is thus whimsical, unpredictable, and so irrational. The genuine play of language thus stands as a refutation of the doctrines of meaning, order, logic, teleology and rationality which is now to be relegated to the epoch of "western metaphysics". We consider finally Foucault.

It might be argued by scholars that Foucault does not belong in this group of thinkers because the notion of play, either in its own right or as a guiding metaphor, plays a far less explicit role in his thinking than was the case with the others. This much is true. Nevertheless, I wish to cite him as a somewhat different sort of confirmation. For even though he does not use the explicit metaphor of play so predominantly, his position contains the same element, the same constellation of ideas, for which the other thinkers use the image of child's play. I refer to a repudiation of a ground or origin where one has long been assumed, to a corresponding repudiation of a telos to the happening of things, and thus to a general repudiation of a "logic" or rationality to history; in short, there is the same appeal to a "without why" doctrine that we have seen previously. If Foucault does not explicitly use "Spiel als Weltsymbol," he might have. In his case, this constellation of ideas centers around his notion of "discursive series," which involved a repudiation of the notions of teleology, origin, and logic to history. These notions are themselves characteristic, according to Foucault, of a specific discursive series (metaphysics) which is now achieving closure. Thus, for example, instead of there being a coherent series of "ages" or "epochs", (the Greek Golden Age, Middle Ages, Renaissance, etc.), each with a set of characteristics which pervades all its aspects (religious, artistic, moral, political, etc.), and each of which arises out of the previous age and leads to the next, there is on the contrary a motley conglomeration of "discursive series", such as that of sexuality, the prison, metaphysics, and even "man". Decisively, these series have no logical connection. They are neither caused by a previous series nor do they cause subsequent series. Neither does a given set of more or less contemporaneous discursive series have any necessary or logical connection. Rather, the happening of discursive series is characterized by discontinuity, irruption, and accident. The conception of history he expouses

> "has questioned the themes of convergence and culmination; it has doubted the possibility of creating totalities. It has led to the individualization of different series, which are juxtaposed to one another, follow one another, overlap and intersect, without one being able to reduce them to a linear schema....The notion of discontinuity assumes a major role in the historical disciplines."[78]

Moreover, his view

> "oppose(s) the search for an original foundation that would make rationality the telos of mankind, and link the whole history of thought to the preservation of this rationality, to the maintenance of this teleology, and to the ever necessary return to this foundation"[79]

Again and more strongly, in an article entitled "Nietzsche, Geneology, and History," Foucault contrasts the older view of history, which sees a "linear development" with an inner "logic," to his notion, adopted from Nietzsche, of "geneology," which recognizes that "the world of speech and desires has known invasions, struggles, plundering, disguises, ploys."[80] His own procedure will thus "discover that truth or being do not lie at the root of what we know and what we are, but the exteriority of accidents."[81]

My point from these few citations should now be clear. Foucault shares with the other thinkers cited a constellation of ideas about the world, history, language, Being, for which, again and again, the image of play is used as a metaphor. But the conception of play appealed to is one clearly modeled after the notion of child´s play and the irrationality and whimsicality which that is taken to entail.

As most of these thinkers would be anxious to agree, this use of the metaphor of play and the conception of play underlying it has decisive consequences. I wish in the next section of this chapter to turn to one particularly decisive issue in order to suggest something of what those consequences are. I refer to the understanding these thinkers develop of the "self" or individual.

II

In my development in Chapter 4 of my own understanding of play as founded in the stance of responsive openness, I tried to show that this stance is not "free-floating" or groundless but itself grounded in a certain conception of the self or individual. This conception, recall, has three facets. First, it is a conception of the individual as both incomplete and overfull. More fully, each of us is characterized on the one hand by the triadic syndrome of being incomplete or partial, recognizing or experiencing that incompleteness, and striving to overcome it, to achieve wholeness. At the same time and notwithstanding the apparent paradox, each of us is characterized by an overfullness, an overflowing quality which, as it were, energizes us, leads us literally to ex-press ourselves, and so is the source of our creativity.[82] Second, the individual´s stance toward the world tends to vacillate between the two poles of dominance and submission, in such a way that each of us _is_ this or that specific vacillation. Third, I argued that the notion of the individual is only coherent as, once again, an almost paradoxical

100

co-presence of monadic and relational tendencies. At the time I tried to show that and how play as responsive openness was founded in each of these dimensions; I shall not repeat those arguments here. However, it might be appropriate as a preparation for what follows to clarify the nature of this "grounding" of play in a certain conception of the individual. Just what is the relation of play to this conception of the individual? Let me begin with a number of alternatives that I reject.

To take perhaps the strongest possible claim, one might argue that if one holds to the view of the individual set out, it necessitates or logically entails the view of play as responsive openness. Such a view is too strong. It is at least possible that there are other conceptions of play which are consistent with this understanding of the individual and which therefore could be coherently held as an alternative to my view. This suggests a second position which I reject as too weak, that the relationship between play as responsive openness and the conception of the individual set out is merely one of consistency. On this view, I would be saying no more than that one <u>can</u> reasonably hold this doctrine of play and this doctrine of the individual, along with, presumably, a number of alternatives. "Grounded" would here mean no more than "consistent with," and it is obvious that I intend a stronger connection than that. So if the relation is weaker than logical necessity but stronger than simply consistency, what is its specific nature? To describe the relation which I have expressed as play being "grounded" in a conception of the individual, it is more appropriate to use a somewhat less technical vocabulary than the formal terminology of logical relation. Preserving for the moment the metaphor of ground, I suggest that play as responsive openness is "natural" to this conception of the individual, that it grows out of it, is sustained, confirmed, enhanced by it. Differently stated, play so interpreted is not merely consistent with this view of the individual but is especially appropriate to it; there is an intimate connection between them which perhaps cannot adequately be expressed by the terminology of formal logic. Once more, the conception of the individual I have espoused invites, calls for, the notion of play as responsive openness, even if it does not demand it.

Perhaps the best way to express this relation is to call it teleological or normative. When Aristotle characterized human being as "the rational animal," he obviously meant neither that all human beings at all times are necessarily rational, nor merely that rationality was consistent with human being as human. He meant rather to assert rationality as the telos of human being; insofar as we most adequately and fully attain to our nature, insofar as we are the best that we can be as human, insofar as we attain our highest actuality (entelecheia), we will be rational. To now adumbrate a position whose own fulfillment can only be achieved in the last chapter of this book, I want to claim the same thing about play and the conception of the individual I have espoused. If and to the extent to which it is true that we are incomplete and overfull, both given to dominance and to submission, both monadic and relational, we will best and most adequately fulfill that nature insofar as we take the stance of responsive openness, and so insofar as we are play-ful in the sense I have developed.

Let us turn now to the connection between the view of play modeled after child's play espoused by the European thinkers just discussed, and certain similarities in their own teachings regarding the human individual or self. I refer to that constellation of positions variously described as the dispersion, destruction, de-subjectivizing, deconstruction, or decentering of the self or individual. I am not claiming that the teachings of these thinkers on this issue are identical. As is well-known, they are often polemical about stating the differences. Rather, I wish to argue that just as there was a common core to their understanding of play which was not negated by the various differences acknowledged, so there is a common strain to their teaching on the individual, notwithstanding the differences. Moreover, the similarity between their teaching on play and on the individual is no accident.

Let me set out the teaching on the individual held in common, then establish its plausibility with some brief documentation. According to a view shared by these thinkers, the very notion of "the individual" is not an eternal truth, not a "natural kind" or "substance", but rather a part of the "ideology" of a tradition which began with the Platonic Socrates and is only recently coming to an end. This tradition espoused a belief in the "category" of the individual as a substantial entity. Whatever the myriad differences in accounts of the nature of the individual, it remained the case that there <u>was</u> a set of beings (human beings) each of which <u>was</u> an individual or a self. Whether the individual was taken to be a specific soul, mind, body, or combination thereof, it was this individual which was the source of "personal identity" through time; it was the basis for the notion of personal responsibility in ethics and morals; it was this individual whose "acts" were either free or determined. So deeply imbued did the "category of the individual" become in the metaphysical tradition that it became difficult if not impossible to think the human situation without it. Of course, there were differences and arguments over the specific nature of the human individual ("human nature"); but there was near complete agreement that there was such a being, the human individual or self.

It is this agreement that the thinkers under consideration reject, each in his own way. As intimated above, they hold instead to doctrines of the "dispersion", "deconstruction", or "decentering" of the individual, all of which amount to this: the "individual" is not a being, not an entity, not "real", but is itself a construction or interpretation by the tradition itself. It is thus not "true", or at least it is only true for that tradition; and that tradition has come or is coming to an end. Part of their task is thus to show the ultimate arbitrariness, contingency, or relativism of that conception. For some initial documentation of this, let us begin once again with the foundational thinker in this "new" tradition, Nietzsche. Nietzsche might seem a strange initial choice, since at least one of the thinkers in question, Heidegger, argues that Nietzsche is less the first of the new epoch than the culmination of the old, of western metaphysics.[83] It is easy to see how one could hold this. Nietzsche´s famous teaching concerning the "overman", especially when espoused by that apparently most radically individualistic of all monadic individuals, Zarathustra, can indeed seem to culminate the traditional teaching concerning the individual. But as others have seen, such is finally an inadequate understanding of Nietzsche´s teaching. We can already see its questionability as early as <u>The Birth of Tragedy</u>. There, to be sure, the notion of the individual is present, but it is located in what Nietzsche there calls the Apollinian tendency, which is explicitly identified as the <u>principium</u>

individuationis.[84] However, it becomes clear that the Apollinian -- and so the principium individuationis -- is not the foundational principle either of the world or of human being. It is rather associated with veils, dreaming, and illusion, and what it veils is the Dionysian _truth_ about the world and human being, a truth at first painful and even intolerable but later consoling, which truth is the denial, even more the annihilation, of the individual in a self-less immersion in the whole.[85] To put this early Nietzschean teaching as bluntly as possible for emphasis: the "individual" is a veil, an illusion, a lie, affirmed in order to hide, or as a way of rendering tolerable, the truth, which is the annihilation of the individual.

Notwithstanding the apparent individuality, even egoism, of Zarathustra, I believe that Nietzsche never abandons this early teaching.[86] It would take an elaborate commentary and interpretation of Thus Spoke Zarathustra to establish this fully; here I shall simply adumbrate the basis for my conviction that the repudiation of the individual is a consistently held Nietzschean doctrine. Perhaps the first sign of this "disarticulation" of the self occurs in Part I, in the section entitled "On the Despisers of the Body". There Zarathustra asserts his conviction that the self or soul is not something "in itself" but is really just the body or "something about the body."

> "But the awakened and knowing say: body
> am I entirely, and nothing else; and the
> soul is only a word for something about
> the body."[87]

Later in the book, Zarathustra is even more explicit; the individual is not a "natural kind" nor an "in-itself", but a creation:

> "First, people were creators; and only in
> later times, individuals. Verily, the
> individual himself is still the most
> recent creation."[88]

Finally, in the notes from Will to Power, Nietzsche becomes polemical about the denial of the self. Two brief passages will establish clearly his position:

> "There exists neither ´spirit´, nor reason,
> nor thinking, nor consciousness, nor soul,

104

nor will, nor truth: all are fictions that
are of no use."[89]

"The ´subject´ is not something given, it is
something added and invented and projected
behind what there is."[90]

Nietzsche   could   hardly   be   more   clear,   nor   more
radical.

Heidegger, as always, is both more sober and less
direct   than   Nietzsche.   Nevertheless, as many of his
students have discerned, there are   clear   indications
of   a   decentering   of   the   self throughout his work.
Here again I shall mention only a few signs, in   order
to establish at least the plausibility of my point.

In the well-known "Dasein-analytic" of Being   and
Time, Heidegger distinguishes between Dasein (or human
being) in its "authentic" moments and Dasein as it   is
"proximally   and   for   the   most   part", wherein it is
"lost" in "Das Man" (translated as "the they").[91] At
least   most   of   the   time, Dasein is   not an individual,
authentic self, but lost in an amorphous   "they-self".
Nevertheless,   one   could   say, at least at the time of
Being   and   Time,   Heidegger   held   that   at   least
occasionally   Dasein   was   authentic   (eigentlich   --
literally "one´s own") and so   a   genuine   individual.
To   an   extent,   this   is   true   although   even   it is
ambiguous.   Dasein, Heidegger insists, is not the same
as   "man"   or an individual person, but is precisely a
relation   to   the world: Da-Sein, "Being-there".   As
such,   the   status   of   the   individual human beings who
presumably   exhibit   or   exemplify   Dasein   is   already
opaque.

This opacity is exacerbated after Being and Time.
In several of his later works, Heidegger turns to the
analysis   of   works   of   art, often   literary   ones.   One
might   think that this investigation would lead him to
a   careful   consideration   of   the   artist, the   individual
in question, as it does, for example, with Sartre.[92]
Quite to the   contrary,   Heidegger   regularly   insists
that   the   individuality   of   the   artist   does   not
matter.[93]   In   perhaps   its   strongest   version,
Heidegger   has   this   to   say   about   the   artist in The
Origin of a Work of Art: "The   artist   is   like   a
channel   which   annihilates itself for the sake of the

105

work."[94]

Later, in _Identity and Difference_, Heidegger
reiterates and radicalizes his insistence that Dasein
is not an entity but a relation: "Man is essentially
the relationship of responding to Being and he is only
this."[95] If this is so, what happens to the self?
What is the status of the individual? If we take
Heidegger seriously here -- and one should always and
only take Heidegger seriously -- man is "only" the
relationship of responding to Being. But if so, then
man can hardly also be a self or individual in any
traditional sense.

A final pointer to Heidegger's "deconstruction"
of the self can be seen in his discussions of
language. For our purposes, the point that needs to
be noted is this: Heidegger repudiates the
traditional notion that human being is a _being_ which
has or _uses_ language -- a _zoon logon echon_, "animal
having language", as Aristotle's famous
characterization has it. It is rather language that
has the primacy here, and human speech is if anything
a derivative of the speech of language rather than the
articulations of specific individuals. Two passages
from different works should establish this point. In
What Is Called Thinking?, Heidegger says, "...it is
not we who play with words, but the nature of language
plays with us."[96] Again, in the shorter piece
entitled "Language", he makes the priority even
clearer: "In its essence, language is neither
expression nor an activity of man. Language
speaks."[97]

Gadamer and Fink are close students of Heidegger,
and it is therefore not surprising that their own
views on the individual contain the same ambiguity as
in Heidegger. In both cases, they finally follow
Heidegger in leaning toward the decentering of the
individual. To cite only their discussions of play,
Gadamer's aforementioned insistence that play is not
an "intentional" characteristic of the player, that it
is wrong to "subjectivize" play by locating its source
in any project of a subject, that play thus "happens"
independently of any players, all point toward the
de-emphasis, if not the de-centering, of the
individual. The same is true of Fink's emphasis on
the notion of "play without a player", as well as his
granting of primacy to play as "world-symbol" over
play as a specifically human phenomenon.[98]

With Foucault and Derrida we return to the straightforward and even polemical repudiation of a "centered" self, which we first saw in Nietzsche. In both thinkers the position is so straightforward as not to be controversial; indeed, the doctrine of the decentering of the self becomes a central tenet of both their teachings. In the case of Foucault, he regularly denies, more forcefully even than Heidegger, that a body of "works" can be grounded in a "unity" called "the author".[99] Most explicitly for our purpose, however, he straightforwardly denies, with Nietzsche, the notion that "man" has any more fundamental status than that of a creation, a creation whose time is coming to an end: "As the archaelogy of our thought easily shows, man is an invention of recent date. And one perhaps nearing its end."[100]

Derrida, just as clearly, tells us in Speech and Phenomena that, contre Husserl, "There is no constituting subjectivity",[101] and moreover that

> "The absence of intuition -- and therefore
> of the subject of intuition -- is not only
> tolerated by speech; it is required by
> the general structure of signification, when
> considered in itself. It is radically
> requisite: the total absence of the subject
> and object of a statement -- the death of
> the writer and/or the disappearance of the
> object he was able to describe -- does not
> prevent a text from meaning something. On
> the contrary, this possibility gives birth
> to meaning as such, gives it out to be heard
> and read."[102]

Whatever their specific differences, then, the thinkers I have discussed share, explicitly or implicitly, both a guiding conception of play construed after the model of irrational child's play and a teaching concerning the decentering of the self. Let me now state what I believe to be the connection between these before moving on to an evaluation of this clearly important and pervasive position. Their position regarding the self could be summarized as the conviction that, as Nietzsche puts it explicitly, the individual or self as a "being" in itself simply does not exist; it is at best an invention, a creation, a fiction. As such, there is in fact no "unity" or unifying being, no synthesizer underlying a given set

107

of acts, appearances, or "texts" which we, presumably
under the influence of the old metaphysics, associate
with an "individual". "I" am not a being underlying
and unifying a set of acts and relations (playing
basketball, writing books, loving a wife, fathering
children, teaching). All there really is are these
acts and relations. "I" am a fiction. These acts and
relations, then, are literally without ground; they
are Ab-grund -- an abyss. To use again a Nietzschean
term, they are in truth a play of forces, subject to
an indefinite number of interpretations none of which
are grounded in a "truth" (presumably "the real me").
They are thus a play of forces in the precise sense of
the term which I have shown they employ: an uncaused,
purposeless, ungrounded, amoral, unpredictable and so
irrational play of forces. But insofar as this
situation characterizes not just the notion of the
individual but the world (or Being, or language, or
history), the same relation holds. The world (or its
substitutes) becomes a play of forces in the exact
same sense: a child playing -- and not at draughts.
Play in the sense interpreted thus becomes an accurate
characterization of the happening of forces which used
to be called the self, and by extension, becomes the
best expression of the way the world is: play as
world-symbol. In turn, the affirmation of play as
world-symbol becomes testimony to one's escaping from
the tradition of "metaphysics" which asserted the real
being of the individual. As Fink says of Nietzsche,
"When Nietzsche grasps Being and Becoming as Spiel, he
no longer stands in the confinement of
metaphysics."[103]

However, I must now say that I do not think this
self-understanding (using the term, of course, "under
erasure" in the Derridean sense) is accurate. Let me
restate what I regard as a more accurate portrayal of
the situation, using terminology established in the
development of my own understanding of play in the
previous chapter. There I established that one way of
understanding the controversy concerning the nature of
the individual, a way at least as old as Plato, was to
ask whether the individual is fundamentally monadic or
relational. My suggestion, recall, was that although
some thinkers in our tradition seem to have opted for
a strong version of one over the other, many of our
greatest minds have insisted, in one way or another,
and however precariously, that the human individual is
both monadic and relational. Now it seems to me that
what the thinkers presently under discussion have

repudiated when they repudiate "the individual" is in fact what I called the monadic individual. And what they have put in its place is not, as they suggest, a "new" view which will start a new discursive series. They have rather substituted a radicalized version of the old view of the individual as relational. Perhaps the most manifest example of this is Heidegger's remark in Identity and Difference that "Man is essentially this relationship of responding to Being, and he is only this."[104] But in the case of the others as well, is not to say that there is nothing but a play of forces to say in effect that there is nothing but relations, and no beings who relate? If so, three points need to be reiterated about this position. First, if there is no self, or alternatively, if there are only relations and no relators, it is difficult to understand what meaning the notion of self-knowledge would have. Are we simply to abandon this quest as a hangover of "metaphysics"? Second, in any case, this view of the individual is hardly a "new" one which constitutes "no longer standing in the confinement of metaphysics" but is part of the metaphysical tradition itself. Third and finally, it is not only part of the metaphysical tradition, it is one-sided. That tradition itself had, by and large, a far richer understanding of the individual as (with some notable exceptions) both monadic and relational. What metaphysics has joined together these thinkers would seem to have torn asunder.

I close this chapter with a brief summation. The conception of play as purposeless, goalless child's play and the conception of the individual as nothing but a play of forces go hand in hand. Both have about them plausibility and value, derivative of the fact that they are part of the truth: one mode (however defective) of play is child's play, and one mode (however partial) of individuality or self-hood is as relational. But both share the same defect, that of radical partiality, as I have attempted to show. We can share with these thinkers a recognition of the significance of finitude and an attraction to "de-totalization" without abandoning the goal to give as comprehensive an account of the human situation as possible. A conception of play founded solely on the paradigm of child's play cannot begin to exhaust the richness and significance of play altogether, and a conception of the individual founded on that conception of play cannot in turn account for the genuine richness of human self-hood. We are ready to return to the development of some of the ramifications of my own conception of play.

Footnotes, Chapter 5

1). Huizinga, Johan, _Homo Ludens: A Study of the Play Element in Culture_, Boston, Beacon Press, 1950, page 3.
2). Ibid.
3). Ibid, page 4.
4). Heidegger, Martin, _Der Satz vom Grund_, Neske, 1957, page 188.
5). Among others, see Suits, Bernard, _The Grasshopper: Games, Life, and Utopia_, Toronto, University of Toronto Press, 1978, Chapters 1-3.
6). Hans, James, _The Play of the World_, Amherst, University of Massachusetts Press, 1981, pages 10, 15.
7). Fink, Eugen, "The Ontology of Play", in _Sport and the Body: A Philosophical Symposium_, eds. Ellen Gerber and Wm. Morgan, Second Edition, Philadelphia, Lea & Febiger, 1979, Page 76.
8). James Hans (op.cit. pages 2 ff.) argues that sports and even traditional examples of play should not be taken as paradigms of play generally. I agree that they should not be taken as exclusive paradigms; but neither should they be ignored, and any position which does ignore them is thereby seriously defective.
9). Heraclitus, Fragment 52, in Diels, Kranz, _Die Fragmente der Vorsokratiker_, Zurich, Weidmann, 1968, volume 1, page 162.
10). Nietzsche, Friedrich, _Philosophy in the Tragic Age of the Greeks_, trans. Marianne Cowan, Chicago, Gateway Editions, 1962, page 62.
11). This is brought out well in an article by David Roochnik, "Competing Paradigms of Play", presented at the annual meeting of the Philosophical Society for the Study of Sport, Western Illinois University, October, 1979.
12). Nietzsche, _Thus Spoke Zarathustra_, in _The Portable Nietzsche_, ed. Walter Kaufmann, New York, Viking Press, 1975, page 123.
13). Ibid, page 139.
14). Ibid, page 178. Nietzsche may be playing on the etymology of the old English, plagen, "to take a risk".
15). Ibid, page 259.
16). Ibid, page 153.
17). Ibid, page 198-199.

18). Ibid, page 278. See also page 309.
19). Fortunately, this case has been established in an excellent way by John Caputo in his article, "Being, Ground, and Play in Heidegger" (Man and World, volume 3, 1971, pages 26-48), and in his book, The Mystical Element in Heidegger's Thought, (Athens, Ohio, Ohio University Press, 1978), so we may be aided by his guidance.
20). Heidegger, Der Satz vom Grund, Neske, 1957.
21). Ibid, page 186.
22). Ibid.
23). Ibid, page 188.
24). Ibid.
25). Heidegger, What Is Called Thinking?, trans. Fred Wieck and Glenn Gray, New York, Harper & Row, 1968, page 118.
26). Ibid, page 119.
27). Caputo, The Mystical Element in Heidegger's Thought, page 58. Hans, op.cit. page 66 ff., also emphasizes the kinship of play and violence.
28). Ibid, page 87.
29). Caputo, "Being, Ground, and Play in Heidegger", page 39.
30). Heidegger, Der Satz vom Grund, page 188.
31). Caputo, The Mystical Element in Heidegger's Thought, page 84.
32). Gadamer, Hans-Georg, Truth and Method, trans. Garrett Barden and John Cumming, New York, Continuum, 1975, page 99.
33). Ibid, pages 96, 97, 98, 102.
34). Ibid, pages 97, 102.
35). Ibid, page 94.
36). Ibid, page 93.
37). Ibid, page 101.
38). Ibid, page 91.
39). Ibid, page 92.
40). Ibid.
41). Ibid.
42). Ibid.
43). Ibid, page 93.
44). Ibid. Hans, op.cit. page 7, 44 is in basic agreement with Gadamer here.
45). Ibid, page 100.
46). Ibid, page 92.
47). Fink, Eugen, Spiel als Weltsymbol, Stuttgart, Kohlhammer Verlag, 1960.
48). Fink, Oase des Glucks: Gedanken zu einer Ontologie des Spiels, Freiburg, Alber-Verlag, 1957. Translated in abridged form as "The

Ontology of Play", in Sport and the Body: A
Philo- Symposium, pages 73-83.I shall cite this
translation.
49). Fink, "The Ontology of Play", page 75.
50). Ibid, page 83.
51). Fink, Spiel als Weltsymbol, page 239.
52). Fink, "The Ontology of Play", page 76.
53). Fink, Spiel als Weltsymbol, page 238.
54). Fink, "The Ontology of Play", page 77.
55). Fink, Spiel als Weltsymbol, page 63. See also
"The Ontology of Play", page 74.
56). Fink, "The Ontology of Play", page 76.
57). Ibid, page 83, Spiel als Weltsymbol, pages
28-29.
58). Fink, Spiel als Weltsymbol, pages 238, 239.
See also "The Ontology of Play", page 76.
59). Fink, Nietzsches Philosophie, Stuttgart,
Kohlhammer, 2nd Edition, 1968, page 188.
60). Fink, Spiel als Weltsymbol, page 62.
61). Ibid, page 239.
62). Fink, "The Ontology of Play", page 77. See
also page 73.
63). Ibid, page 77.
64). Fink, Spiel als Weltsymbol, pages 15-16.
65). Ibid, page 32.
66). Ibid, pages 64-66 et al. See also "The
Ontology of Play", pages 79-83.
67). Fink, "The Ontology of Play", page 79.
68). Ibid, page 82.
69). Ibid.
70). Camus, Albert, Resistance, Rebellion, and
Death, New York, Alfred Knopf Inc., 1961, page
242.
71). Fink, Spiel als Weltsymbol, pages 93, 233, et
al.
72). Derrida, Jacques, L'ecriture et la Difference,
Paris, 1967, page 427. Translated as Writing
and Difference, Alan Bass, trans., Chicago,
University of Chicago Press, 1978, page 292.
73). Ibid, page 423.
74). Derrida, Of Grammatology, trans. Gayatri
Chakravorty Spivak, Baltimore, Johns Hopkins
University Press, 1976, page 6.
75). Ibid, page 7.
76). Ibid, page 57.
77). Ibid, page 50.
78). Foucault, Michel, The Archaeology of Knowledge,
trans. A.M.S. Smith, New York, Harper Colophon
Books, 1972, page 8.
79). Ibid, page 13.

80). Foucault, "Nietzsche, Geneology, History", in
Language, Counter-Memory, Practice: Selected
Essays and Interviews, ed. and trans. Donald
Bouchard and Sherry Simon, Ithaca, Cornell
University Press, 1977, page 139.

81). Ibid, page 146.

82). See Hans, op.cit. pages 5, 55, 63, for his own
discussion of this phenomenon.

83). His central claim in Nietzsche I and Nietzsche
II.

84). Nietzsche, The Birth of Tragedy, trans. Walter
Kaufmann, New York, Vintage Books, 1967, page
36 ff.

85). Ibid, pages 40, 49, 50, 60, 67, et al.

86). For excellent documentation see the article by
J. Hillis Miller, "The Disarticulation of the
Self in Nietzsche", in Monist, vol. 64, no. 2,
April, 1981, pages 247-261.

87). Nietzsche, Thus Spoke Zarathustra, in The
Portable Nietzsche, page 146.

88). Ibid, page 171.

89). Nietzsche, The Will to Power, trans. Kaufmann
and Hollingdale, New York, Random House, 1967,
page 266.

90). Ibid, page 267.

91). Heidegger, Being and Time, trans. Macquarrie &
Robinson, New York, Harper & Row, 1962, see
especially Part I, sections IV and V.

92). Sartre, Jean-Paul, Essays in Aesthetics,
trans. Wade Baskin, New York, Washington Square
Press, 1966.

93). See for example, "The Origin of a Work of Art",
and "Language", both in Poetry, Language,
Thought, trans. Albert Hofstadter, New York,
Harper & Row, 1971 pages 40, 195.

94). Ibid, page 40 (my alterations in translation).

95). Heidegger, Identity and Difference, trans. Joan
Stambaugh, New York, Harper Torchbooks, 1969,
page 31.

96). Heidegger, What is Called Thinking?, pages
118-119.

97). Heidegger, Poetry, Language, Thought, page 197.

98). It must be noted again that Fink does not
entirely abandon the notion of the self or
individual, at least if we can take his words
in their precise sense. Recall that in "The
Ontology of Play", he speaks of play as a
"passion of the soul" (page 77).

99). See Foucault, The Archaeology of Knowledge,
pages 23-24.

100). Foucault, The Order of Things, New York,
      Pantheon Books, 1970, page 387.
101). Derrida, Speech and Phenomena, trans. David
      Allison, Evanston, Northwestern University
      Press, 1973, pages 84-85n.
102). Ibid, pages 92-93.
103). Fink, Nietzsches Philosophie, page 188. See
      also Reiner Schurmann, "The Ontological
      Difference and Political Philosophy", in
      Philosophy and Phenomenological Research,
      vol. XL, no. 1, September, 1979, page 102:
      Eckhart and Nietzsche, as precursors of the new
      "post-humanist" epoch, "suggest the abolition
      of teleology in action; they recommend action
      ´without why´, without end or purpose. In this
      tradition, the paradigm of action is play".
104). Heidegger, Identity and Difference, page 31.

Chapter 6: Competition, Friendship, and Risk-Taking

Perhaps a brief review of the structure of the preceeding chapters will be helpful as an introduction to this chapter. In Part I, I considered some of the major disciplines whose representatives have studied play (sociology, psychology, history), with an eye to seeing both what sorts of contributions each can make to an understanding of play, as well as what the limitations of each are. In Part II, I developed my own version of a philosophical understanding of play, centering around the stance of responsive openness. In the previous chapter, I confronted my view with what I consider the most important alternative conception of play.

In the present chapter, I wish to take up a number of themes which I believe any adequate understanding of play must consider. I hope to show that my own view of play can both make sense of and shed light on these themes, these satellites in any constellation of play. I do not intend, however, that they will be exhaustive; to exhaust the themes which derive from or are centrally related to play would border on an "infinite task". I will consider three such themes: competition, friendship, and risk-taking. As we shall see, they themselves are closely connected. One might note immediately that none of these three are present in all play. Competitive play, especially sports, is clearly only one form of play, however pervasive and important it is. Friendship is evidently not always present in our play -- sometimes quite the contrary. And to say the least, playing solitaire, tittley-winks, or charades would hardly rank in anyone´s list of activities under the heading "living dangerously". It is for this reason that I refer to these themes as satellites of play rather than essential attributes of any and all play, and it is for this reason that I now consider them in a separate chapter from my setting out of the stance of play itself. Still, satellites are intimately connected to the planet around which they revolve; so here, once again, these three themes often arise in our play and both shed light on and are illuminated by play itself. Moreover, my consideration of these themes will hopefully serve as an example of how other issues related to play might be tied in with the nature of play itself and the humans who play.

I would suppose that nearly everyone who has participated in competitive sports, from sand-lot games through the more organized level of high school and college teams to professional athletics, has had one version or another of the following two experiences.[1] On the one hand, we have experienced that situation in which our competitive play breaks down into alienation. This can take on a variety of forms and degrees of intensity. It can be as mild as a slight feeling of irritation when we feel that our opponent has hit us, or perhaps hit a ball at us, harder than he or she needed to. Or it can be the stronger and more pervasive feeling which some of us have that we "do better" in competitive sports when we are angry at our opponents, that somehow this spurs us on so that we "really want to win." It can show itself at those times when we hurt someone in competitive play, yet instead of feeling apologetic or at least sympathetic towards our injured opponent, we find ourselves exhilarated. At its extreme form within the context of sports, the game actually degenerates into fisticuffs. In all such cases as these, we have that co-presence of competition and alienation which is so common that it has led some to see a causal relation: competition <u>causes</u> alienation. Anyone who has never experienced one form or another of alienation in their competitive play has had an extraordinarily fortunate - not to say sheltered - sporting experience.

But there is a second kind of competitive experience which most of us have also had, one very different from the latter. I refer to that experience of competitive play in which our relation to our opponent can be that mode of positive encounter which deepens into a form of friendship. Many of our closest friends are people whom we "get to know" in competitive situations, (not to mention the myriad ways in which non-competitive play can be an occasion of friendship). For many of us, playing sports with someone is a way of preserving and deepening an established friendship. Sometimes we can even say that "I never play harder than against my friend," yet even this greater intensity enhances rather than diminishes the positive strength of the relationship. I note with interest that there is less disposition to attribute a causal relation here between competition and friendship; we are rarely informed that competition causes friendship. Still, anyone who has never experienced this sort of friendship in competitive play has had an extraordinarily unfortunate -- not to say perverse -- sporting experience.

Now the point of these remarks is to enable me to establish what I take to be an obvious but strangely controversial beginning: the empirical news is that both alienation and friendship sometimes accompany competitive play. This raises a set of questions upon which we need to reflect. First, can we speak of a causal relation between either competitive play and alienation or competitive play and friendship? If neither, what then is the nature of their respective relations? If both, how can competition be causally tied to such apparently opposite phenomena as alienation and friendship? For that matter, is the direction of the causal relation reversed, that is, do either alienation or friendship <u>cause</u> competition?[2] It is important to reiterate that despite the empirical presence of both alienation and friendship in the competition of play, there is and has been a strong tendency to associate competition closely with alienation, and to regard friendship as in tension not just with alienation but with competition itself. Because the relation between competition and friendship is less obvious and perhaps less prevalent, I shall focus on that relation, though I hope my remarks will be germane to a reflection on the relation of competition and alienation as well.

A second question raised by the co-presence of friendship and alienation in competitive play is this; since both do sometimes occur in play, it would seem to follow that our competitive play ever and again <u>risks</u> alienation. Moreover, a moments reflection reveals to us that much of our play is shot through with a variety of risks, from physical injury to the psychological risks of losing. What is the broader significance of this risk-taking element in our play?

I wish to make it clear immediately that these questions are by no means peculiar to the play situation. The relation of competition and alienation, competition and friendship, competition and risk-taking, these are issues of human being itself. At the same time, as I have argued elsewhere,[3] the play situation, by its natural intensity and its (sometimes arbitrary) delimitation in space, time, and purpose, can make certain themes more visible than in our ongoing everyday lives. To be sure, play and playful competition can without doubt be engaged in for their own sake; that is compatible with my conviction that the foundational issues of play are not limited to play itself. We need to continue our effort to show how play and human being are mutually implicated, and see how they shed light on each other. Let me begin with the following considerations.

The view has been stated by many a philosopher that human beings are "by nature" competitive, by which is usually meant that in one way or another, whether in our business dealings, or our creative projects, our play or our love affairs, the "competitive instinct" will eventually show itself. Moreover, this thesis, when it is set out with care, seems usually to be coupled with a second thesis about the natural alienation of human beings. Thus Hobbes speaks of the "state" of "nature" as a "war of all against all,"[4] and Hegel, in his famous account of the development of self-consciousness in the Phenomenology of Spirit, speaks of a primordial "fight to the death" arising out of the desire for recognition.[5] In perhaps its most popular version, Marx, who does not accept the teaching that human being is by nature competitive and alienated, still preserves such a close connection between the two that he argues that the removal of competition - through the overcoming of capitalism - will bring about the abolition of alienation.[6]

On the other hand, there is another thesis about human being, usually associated with romanticism, that argues that human beings are by nature friendly or loving, that only the perversions of society or history bring about the rise of competition or alienation.[7] Significantly, the view that human beings are naturally friendly is usually contrasted to the view that we are by nature competitive.

We need, then, to ask, is it the case that there is a necessary connection between human being as competitive and alienation? Or is there a conception of human being which would allow that we be, in a sense, both by nature competitive and by nature given to friendship? I wish to suggest that there is indeed such a conception, and moreover, that human play is just the theatre where that complex nature gets most visibly manifested. It is the conception of human being elaborated in Part II.

Let me begin by recalling two conceptions of the individual which, once again, are usually taken as in tension if not utterly opposed. I refer to what I earlier called, respectively, the monadic and the relational. Briefly, the spokesmen for the monadic conception of the individual argue that human being is - or at least should be - an autonomous, self-reliant monad, whose essence, literally whose being, is intrinsic. To be sure, such individuals will enter into relations with others. But such relationships as people enter will not on this view be literally essential to our nature. Our relations with others may please us, trouble us, amuse or bore us. But they will not make us what we are. I will not go into the history and documentation of this view since it has already been presented in Part II. Let me emphasize here that the spokesmen for this conception present it as desirable, sometimes even as an ideal; and indeed, most of us do experience this sense of autonomy as a positive one. Conversely, we often are troubled when we feel our relations with others to be what we disparagingly call "dependency relationships."

According to the spokesmen for the relational individual, we are relational by nature. We are what we are and who we are, positively or negatively, in terms of the name and nature of our relations with others. For example, at the level of social role definition, if I am a father, husband, teacher, and athlete, these definitive roles all refer to modes of relations with others. I want to emphasize that the difference between this view and the former does not depend on whether or not we do relate to others, but on how essential those relations are to our being. As in the case of the monadic individual, so here, the adherents to this view in nearly all cases affirm it, see it not only as the natural way for humans to be but as desirable and something to be perpetuated. Indeed the appeal of participatory involvements, from team sports to nationalism, would hardly be understandable if the conception of the individual as relational did not contain some truth.

We need now to ask after the relationship, if any, between these conceptions of the individual on the one hand and on the other the themes of competition, alienation, and friendship which are central to the present reflection. I would submit that the conception of the individual as monadic typically and most easily develops an understanding of

121

human being in which competition is present and tends toward alienation, whereas the relational view more easily develops a version of natural friendship, either as original or as a goal. It is not difficult to cite as _prima_ _facie_ evidence for these associations some of the examples from Part II. There is a clear relation between the monadic conception of the individual and the competition of capitalism for Adam Smith, who in order to claim that some good will emerge from this situation is forced to the somewhat desperate expedient of the "invisible hand".[8] Nietzsche, who sometimes seems to argue for the monadic view, accepts and even affirms alienation as part of the life of genuinely creative individuals[9]. Again, Marx draws a clear connection between the abolition of alienation under capitalism and the fulfillment of the relational ideal of species being.[10] Finally, the connection between the relational view and a natural tendency to friendship can be seen in Buber's fundamental thesis that the I-thou relation is the highest possibility for human being.[11] If this is plausible, then we must note immediately that the oppositional character of our subject seems to have been deepened. Natural competition and alienation seem grounded in a conception of the individual as monadic, natural friendship in the individual as relational, and these two conceptions seem on the surface opposed.

But we have already seen that many, myself included, have been unsatisfied with this initial opposition. Because both have their appeal, because most of us when we reflect upon it want to consider ourselves both monadic, with its connotations of autonomy and authenticity, and relational, with its connotations of community and participation, efforts have been made again and again to argue that the opposition is not irreconcilable, that human being is both monadic and relational, a position which I defended in Part II. If indeed the monadic and relational conceptions of the individual are reconcilable, what does this suggest about the relationship between competition and alienation on the one hand, which we earlier associated with the monadic individual, and friendship on the other, which we connected most fundamentally with relational individuality? Evidently, it suggests a closer relation than at first appeared. The problem is to work it out adequately.

122

At this point, I wish to remind the reader of my attempt in Part II to show that the understanding of human being as monadic/relational is connected to several others. I refer, first, to the understanding of human being as incomplete yet at once overfull and overflowing, and second, the view of humans as forever vacillating between a stance of dominance and a stance of submission. I tried to show how all three views, however strange or even paradoxical they may seem in themselves, could be related to my conception of play as responsive openness. With these points in mind, we may now be prepared to relate them to the possible reconciliation of competition and friendship.

Let us begin with competition. Consider first the original meaning of the word. Com-petitio means "to question together, to strive together". Immediately we see that according to the original meaning of the word, competition is not necessarily connected to alienation; instead, it is easily tied to the possibility of friendship. It is a questioning of each other together, a striving together, presumably so that each participant achieves a level of excellence that could not have been achieved alone, without the mutual striving, without the competition. Two very common examples should make this clear. The first is the observation, so well-known as to have become almost a cliché, that good teams or good players usually play more excellently when the competition is most challenging, and conversely, that playing against a poor team or player all too often results in a "bad game". The second example will be familiar to all parents. I remember watching with delight the milestone in my own children's growth, when they began to see the real point of competition. When very young, they would do their best to "stack the sides" of sand-lot games in their favor, to arrange the game so that they would win by the largest possible margin ("We won 56 to nothing!"), and so in fact that there would be as little competition as possible. For them, indeed, "winning wasn't everything, it was the only thing". Very gradually, however, they began to see beyond this, to see that the games were actually more fun, more exciting, when the teams were well-matched. They began to make up sides now so that the teams would be as even as possible, so that the outcome of the game would be genuinely in question. They had seen the point; they now wanted the competition, wanted the challenge of equal competitors. We find the same sense in the related word "con-test", a testing together, where again the notion of togetherness suggests cooperation which points much more naturally to friendship than to alienation.[12] There are, of course, related words which do suggest the elements of alienation. Perhaps the most obvious is "opposition," in which we posit ourselves against the other, a characterization which clearly makes space for alienation. It is as if the elemental words developed for our play situation indicate the possibility both of alienation and of friendship as naturally tied to play. For our purposes, what we need to emphasize is that competition in its root meaning suggests an affinity more with friendship than with alientation.

Now of course, etymological meanings, though instructive, hardly would be sufficient alone to establish this philosophic point. But there are at least two other considerations which suggest that the connection between competition and friendly cooperation is no etymological accident. First, I would remind the reader of what we could call the existential evidence adduced at the beginning of this chapter. From time to time, friendship does arise and is even deepened within the context of competition. To be sure, this establishes no causal relation, but it does tstify clearly to the compatibility of the two, and establishes at least the possibility of a closer connection. It is clearly commensurate, for example, with the older conception of friendship as a "demand relationship," wherein friends, far from "not hassling" each other or letting each other "do their own thing," exhibit their friendship through the constant if implicit demand that each be the best that he or she can be. Competition manifestly can be a mode of this form of friendship.

Second, the considerations earlier proposed concerning the relation between responsive openness, play, and the respective human dualities of monadic/relational, incomplete/overfull, and dominance/submission, offer a kind of ontological evidence, or perhaps better, an ontological framework within which we can understand that and how competition and friendship, though not necessarily in a causal relation, are nevertheless intimately connected. Competition is a questioning or striving together. Its energy, force, striving, is grounded in our sense of incompleteness and striving for fulfillment. Here, however, the sense in which

124

striving for fulfillment is enhanced by and with others is made explicit. In competition we become more than we were, we often attain new heights of excellence in a given activity. All too often, we are tempted to credit that achievement to ourselves alone, or to those explicitly involved in cooperation with us, such as teammates or coaches. But we also know, upon reflection, that our competitors are often critical to our achievement of excellence. As the traditional handshake at the end of a game truly symbolizes, we have our competitors <u>to thank</u> for offering us that occasion in which we might have transcended ourselves. In competing with others, our chances for fulfillment are seen as occurring within a framework of positive involvement with others. We may indeed "play our hearts out" "against" our competitors. But in the deepest sense, it is a cooperation. If friendship is a demand relation, then our competitors should be our friends, for they may lead us to be the best we can; by playing hard, they ask that of us, they demand it of us. Far from being opposed, then, competition and friendship are seen as founded together in our natures as incomplete/overfull, monadic/relational.

At the beginning of this chapter, I asked after the relation between competition and friendship, competition and alienation. I specifically wondered whether that relationship was causal. The gist of these reflections is to incline me to answer, no. Competition <u>causes</u>, in the sense of efficient causality, neither friendship nor alienation, nor vice-versa. That is not the accurate statement of the relation. Nor is it adequate merely to say they are compatible, that competition is occasionally accompanied by friendship (or alienation). I have argued that the relationship is more intimate than that, that both are founded together in our nature as incomplete/overfull and monadic/relational. Let me now try to specify that relation. What I am pointing toward, once again, is a teleological relation between competition and friendship. Competition, as a striving or questioning together towards excellence, <u>in so far as it most adequately fulfills its possibilities</u>, does so as a mode of friendship. To state it differently, the apotheosis or highest version of competition is as friendship. Moreover, like all good teleologists, I hold the <u>highest</u> possibility to be the truly <u>natural</u> situation, in the light of which other manifestations of competition, specifically that of alienation, are to be judged defective. According, then, to my teleological account of competitive play, all competitive play which fails to attain its highest possibility, that of friendship, must be understood as a "deficient mode" of play. This could even be interpreted as implying an ethical injunction: we <u>ought</u> to strive at all times to let our competitive play be a mode of friendship.

Now of course, this happy state of affairs can and does break down all too regularly. Our "competition", we could now say, devolves into "opposition", and we experience the common co-presence of alienation and play. Why does such alienation occur? There are no doubt myriad reasons, ranging from the personal psychology of the participants, even our moods and the events immediately preceding our play, to social convention (it is obviously more acceptable to have fights in hockey games than in basketball games; indeed, one sometimes gets the feeling it is socially expected). The point of the preceding remarks is to establish that it is not natural, teleologically, that competition lead to alienation; we need not accept it as "part of what competition is", and thus by accepting it implicitly affirm its presence, warrant its perpetuation. Alienation may accompany competitive play at least as often as friendship. It is also true that a minute percentage of all acorns develop into oak trees; that does not deny that becoming an oak tree is the <u>telos</u>, the natural fulfillment, of an acorn. So it is with competition and friendship. The best, the highest, competition occurs in the mode of friendship, even though almost every instance of competitive play involves us in the risk of alienation.

This leads us to the second of the questions we raised at the outset of this chapter, the question of the risk-taking element in competitive play. There is something strange about this propensity for risk-taking in our play. In the previous chapter, we considered a number of important thinkers who regarded play as fundamentally irrational. That view is shared by many who are not professional philosophers, and one of the "irrational" elements often attributed to play is its risk-taking propensity. Consider for the moment this line of thought.

Most of us most of the time consider ourselves to be reasonable people, consider it desirable to be rational, and strive to be so. Among the many connotations of this term is presumably this, that we do not take needless risks. Indeed, taking needless risks is usually interpreted as a sure sign of irrationality. I do not cross the street without looking both ways; and if I do, that is a sign that I am being self-destructive. I do not invest a large proportion of my money in fly-by-night organizations which may make me a millionaire but will more likely break me. I do not get married unless I am reasonably sure that the depth of our feeling for each other is such that our relationship is likely to be enduring. In short, the attitude of our culture generally toward risk-taking is that unnecessary risk-taking is a sign of irrationality. To be sure, we all occasionally must take risks; as part of our self-development, we must from time to time "go out on our own". To take a more extreme example, if I see a child drowning in a lake during a thunderstorm, there is perhaps a moral sense in which I "must" risk my life to save him or her. Yes, to be sure, life is like that; we occasionally come across situations which demand that we take risks. But to respond to situations which demand risk-taking is one thing; to invite risks, to willingly and even enthusiastically seek out situations which involve risk-taking, that is altogether different, surely testimony that a person is at least sub-consciously suicidal. Yet that is precisely what occurs again and again in our play.

At the risk of dwelling on the obvious, let me delineate some of the risks not just occasionally but regularly involved in play and even, as I shall argue, central to its attraction. Surely the most manifest is the risk of physical injury. All contact sports involve a risk of injury so prevalent as to amount to an expectation, but it is hardly limited to contact sports. Having played basketball all my life I expected that running, which I recently have taken up, would be relatively injury free. I now know otherwise, though I am no more tempted to give up running merely because I am constantly sore than I was to give up basketball the first time I sprained my ankle or had a tooth knocked out by a flying elbow. The most extreme examples here would probably be those sports such as rock climbing or automobile racing which involve the genuine risk not just of injury but of death.[13] But there are other kinds of risk involved than that of physical injury. As Arnold Beisser, in his book, The Madness In Sport[14] has documented so well, our play, and especially our competitive play, is pervaded by psychological risk. Most obvious, perhaps, is the fear many of us have of losing, and the effect that has on our egos. All too many of us consider ourselves somehow diminished as persons when we lose. Indeed, we are often encouraged to feel that way by misguided coaches. But as Beisser documents, we may also, for complex reasons, fear winning as well. In addition, many of us are reluctant to take up new sports, especially when those sports involve skills that take time to develop, for fear of "looking like a fool". How many people have hesitated to take up skiing, or even road running, for this reason? Clearly, this too is a psychological risk.

A third kind of risk, already discussed, shows itself clearly in all competitive sports, the risk that what begins as a friendly contest may degenerate into alienation. Relatively few of us enjoy being alienated from others. Most of us, quite reasonably, do what we can to avoid situations where alienation is likely to ensue. Yet a person would have to be naive not to realize that the situation in competitive play, whether it be because of the intensity of the contest, the desire to win, the physical contact, or other factors, is one shot through with the risk of alienation.

Now there may well be other kinds of risk involved in play. My purpose here is not exhaustively to catalogue the modes of risk but to establish that risk-taking of some form is a decisive and ever-present element in many forms of play. If so, we are faced with this question: especially in the light of the considerations adduced a moment ago, does not this establish once and for all that play is, as we have seen argued, irrational? To the extent that we desire to be rational, should we not therefore avoid play when possible, play only as much as our irrational neuroses for risk-taking demand? If not, why do we play, and why ought we to play?

What especially interests me here is again not so much the possibility of psychological or sociological answers to these questions as what I earlier called ontological responses. Let me explain once more. One might well respond to the questions I have asked by

128

relatively instance-specific hypotheses founded on psychological or sociological assumptions. John takes these risks because, being much smaller than most men, he feels the need to show that he is a "real man." Mary takes these risks because she is an active feminist and anxious to show that women have guts too. Hobart does it because his name is Hobart. Now without denying the possible correctness of such explanations, I do not feel that they go far enough. One needs to ask, what is human being like, that a man like John would feel the need to overcome small stature by risk-taking, that Mary would feel the need to show that her femininity does not exclude courage in the face of risks, that Hobart would feel the need to overcome the name "Hobart"? Here we arrive at the more fundamental but more general question which I have termed ontological: what is it about being human that might lead us to take risks, even when they are unnecessary? Can such apparent irrationality be founded in, and perhaps even justified by, human nature itself, as we saw was the case with competition?

I wish to suggest that it can, and that it can by an appeal once again to these dualities of human being which I introduced in Part II: human being as monadic/relational, as incomplete/overfull, and as vacillating between dominance/submission. Let me develop the point in a somewhat different way. In Part II, I suggested that the responsiveness of responsive openness was grounded in that aspect of our natures as overflowing, while the openness of responsive openness in turn was grounded in our incompleteness or partiality. I would like now to give that a somewhat different slant by appealing to one of the most clear manifestations of this connection in human behavior, the phenomenon of the question. Consider, for a moment what we might call the stance of questioning. When we question something or someone, we testify by that very act to our incompleteness or openness. That is, we only question genuinely when we do not know, when we lack knowledge, and so in that decisive sense are incomplete. At the same time, the very act of questioning is itself responsive, or a sign of our fullness or power. Instead of merely accepting - passively -- our incomplete state, or the first answer that comes along, we question, and we move thereby to overcome that incompleteness; we respond to it. Questioning, we might thus say, is a paradigm case of responsive

129

openness, grounded in our nature as incomplete/overflowing.

There is a mode of questioning particularly germane to the phenomenon of risk-taking: the questioning of oneself. To be sure, one way in which self-questioning manifests itself is in the explicit questioning of ourselves. We often enough, or perhaps not often enough, ask questions of ourselves, of our motives, our actions, our natures, as part of the movement toward self-knowledge. In my final chapter I shall turn explicitly to this decisive issue through a consideration of the relation of self-knowledge and play. Here, however, we need to note that explicit asking questions of oneself is not the only form which our self-questioning takes. We can also question ourselves -- often in a way every bit as profound as explicitly asking questions -- by calling ourselves into question through our actions. We call ourselves into question, we "put ourselves on the line." How? Often enough, precisely by taking risks. Risk-taking situations are occasions in which what kind of people we are is literally held open to question, indeed, in which we find out who we are in the midst of becoming who we are. Far from being unnatural or irrational activities, then, those situations in which we take risks, our play foremost among them, are occasions in which we exhibit our natures. They are quite literally natural things to do. Sometimes, as we know, these moments of risk-taking can be moments of self-knowledge in the literal sense. But as I hope is now clear, explicit self-knowledge is but one of the ways in which risk-taking can occasion that calling into question of ourselves in which we become more than what we were, in which our natural striving gets exhibited.

But even if risk-taking is thus grounded in human nature, and explicable in that sense, it presumably remains the case that at least some risk-taking is irrational. Indeed, as my earlier examples from everyday life testify, incomplete or not we are in the habit of avoiding unnecessary risks and recommending the same to others. Yet there seems to be something about the play situation which, coupled with the considerations set forth so far, "frees us" to take risks, perhaps to justifiably take risks, which we otherwise avoid. If we could account for this, we would contribute to an ontological response both to the question "why do we play?" and also to the question "why _ought_ we to play?" Differently stated, we would have an ontological account which is at once teleological, in which the account of the nature of things includes an account of why that nature ought to be the way it is. What, then, might the other element or elements involved be? I wish first to suggest one which strikes me as decisive: the phenomenon of trust, a quality perhaps integral to the very possibility of play.

Let me establish the initial connection between trust and risk-taking by some negative examples. Racing car drivers, as is well-known, are a very close knit group. They are extremely suspicious of new-comers, and quite publically wary of them until they "prove themselves." What does it mean to "prove oneself" in this context? Win a few big races? Not at all. Or again, suppose you are playing squash with an opponent who in the course of the match, happens to whack you hard in the leg while ostensibly going for a ball. Instead of apologizing or at least expressing concern for your injury, your opponent turns away with an ill-concealed smile on his face. How playful will the rest of the match be? Or, finally, suppose you are a high school football coach, dedicated to teaching your players this rough, tough game you love in a fair way that always stays within the spirit and letter of the rules. You learn that the opposing coach has been teaching rake-blocking to his players, in which they ram their face masks into the chest of the oppposing player, then rake it up abruptly under his chin, often causing injury. How will this affect your feelings about the up-coming game?

In all three examples, we begin with a situation already full of risk. Race car driving is dangerous under the best of conditions. Playing squash or football involves the risk of injury even when the spirit and letter of the rules are followed. What brings on the reluctance and suspicion in the examples, then, is not the unwillingness to risk injury _per se_. The participants have already indicated their willingness to take such risks by entering the sport in the first place. Nor do the examples suggest that we willingly risk minor injuries but not major ones; certainly car racing, but other sports as well, involve the risk of life itself. Rather, the examples show an altogether different parameter within which we are willing to take risks in our play, and outside of which we are reluctant or

131

suspicious. That parameter is trust. Our willingness and enthusiasm for risk-taking play seems tied to an atmosphere wherein we are involved in a relationship of trust with the other participants. In the case of the car-racing example, it is trust in the other driver's basic ability as a driver; in the squash example, trust that one's opponent is not <u>trying</u> to injure you (although of course he or she may), in the case of the football coach, trust that the opposition has the same basic values and priorities which inform your own involvement in the game. I believe we can generalize from these examples, and say that we find in almost all our play which involves risk-taking a curious co-presence of risk-taking and trust, and that it is this trust in our participants' intentions which is the decisive factor in whether and to what extent we are willing to take such risks. One might even go further and suggest, with an appeal to the same sorts of examples, that without that trust, one is no longer genuinely <u>playing</u>, whatever behavioral resemblance your activity might have to play situations. The case of professional football is instructive here. Many have argued that that activity is no longer play, indeed no longer sport or athletics. Perhaps part of the reason for this is that the basic element of trust among the opposing players has broken down. No longer able to trust that certain players in the game will avoid <u>trying</u> to hurt you, you can no longer <u>play</u> with them in any meaningful sense.

I wish to bring home how striking, even uncanny I find this co-presence of trust and risk-taking in our play. Do we not usually associate trust with that sense of security which <u>eliminates</u> risk, and do we not think of risk-taking as precisely stepping into the sphere of the untrustworthy? "You can trust your car to the man who wears the star." "Go to C.B.T., the bank you can trust". Apparently not, at least in our play (but I suspect not only in our play). Apparently, the line that divides those risks which we are willing to take from those which we are not, which we indeed consider irrational, that line is drawn not at a certain <u>amount</u> of risk, but at the presence or absence of trust. If that trust is present, we willingly take all manner of risks, even of our lives. Without that trust, we are unwilling to risk so much as a bruised leg. I wonder at this. If the presence of trust did indeed eliminate the risk, there would be nothing wonderful. But evidently it does not. What then is there about this trust which makes us willing to take risks which, without its presence, we would avoid as irrational?

One might suggest that there are different kinds of risks, qualitative rather than quantitative distinctions in risks, that need to be drawn. Thus we seem less willing, even within the risk-taking context of sport, to take risks which hinge on the incompetence of the other participants (the race-driving example) or on their malicious intentions (the squash example), or on their incompatible values and priorities (the case of the football coach). There are no doubt other limiting factors which other examples would show. What do they share? I tentatively suggest this: it seems that what we want is to enter risk-taking situations where the risk is as purely as possible one of <u>chance</u>, of the fates. It may well happen that in a car race with competent drivers there will be a serious accident; I will "chance" that, but not in a race with a bunch of incompetents who make an accident all the more likely. I may indeed get injured or injure my opponent in a squash match; I'll chance that, but not if he or she is <u>trying</u> to hurt me. My players may indeed get hurt in next week's football game; I'll chance that, but not if their coach is willing to do anything in order to win. The subtle difference seems to be something like this, that we want to enter into precarious situations, situations where there are risks which cannot be controlled or eliminated in advance. But they must be genuinely left to chance. We seem to set up situations where the preventable risks, or perhaps better, those risks whose source is something other than chance, are eliminated; it is here that trust is so essential. <u>Then</u>, we enthusiastically take risks. To be sure, social conditions, such as playing on an organized team for a school or city, may bring pressures to bear which lead us to continue our participation in the game even when this trust has broken down. But then, obviously, the game has become alienated, and thus, as I have argued, a defective mode of play. My point here is, play that we engage in willingly and enthusiastically is usually informed by trust.

A second and perhaps more obvious factor that enables us to cut down on the preventable risks - and thereby open up the space for that risk-taking that we do seek in play - is knowledge. The point can perhaps be made best by reference to a curious exaggeration

133

prevalent among those who participate in especially dangerous, risk-full sports. When asked about the risks involved in mountain climbing, or sky-diving, or auto racing, whether the questioner be an admirer full of implicit praise or a skeptic whose questions are heavy with implicit accusation of madness, the response is typically the same. "There's not really that much risk for me. For you, yes, it would be an insane risk. But that's because you don't know what you're doing. I know what I'm doing, so it's not really risky." Alvarez, in the previously cited article, quotes from Sterling Moss, the race car driver, as follows:

> "It doesn't frighten me to go over the
> blind brow of a hill at one hundred and
> sixty or seventy miles an hour. I know
> I shall make it. I say to myself, if I
> say anything, that I know how to do this."[15]

Alvarez himself concludes about his own sport of mountain climbing,

"I would rather commit myself 10 times over to El Capitan than go alone into Harlem or Watts, or try to cross Central Park after dark; on a mountain at least you have some control over disaster."[16]

Now these are exaggerations. Knowledge or no knowledge, car racing, mountain climbing, and dozens of other such sports are full of risks. It is a safe prediction indeed that if all the risks were eliminated those activities would soon lose their appeal to the skilled participants. Still, the exaggeration is an exaggeration of the truth. Knowledge in these situations does cut down on the risks. It is perhaps not irrational for Alvarez to climb El Capitan, but it would certainly be madness for me to do so; and the relevant difference between us is that he knows what he is doing whereas I do not.

There are in fact at least two kinds of knowledge that are relevant here. The first and most obvious is the technical knowledge of the skills required in the given sport, the equipment needed, and when to use it. Such knowledge clearly cuts down on the risks involved; it is perhaps what I most acutely lack in mountain climbing, and what would thus make my attempt to climb El Capitan an act of madness rather than a challenging adventure. It is this kind of knowledge which gives us a sense of control over the situation, and with that control the confidence that the risks are worth taking, rational risks rather than irrational ones. The second mode of knowing I shall call familiarity. Recall if you can the first time you went camping in the wilderness, the first time you swam in water over your head, or that you played or spoke before a large audience. That experience was probably filled with fears which were really derivative of your unfamiliarity with the situation. Your lack of confidence was probably overcome as you became more familiar with the situation. Thus the experience of having "been there before," whether on a mountain face, near a coral reef, or before a large audience, furnishes us with that knowledge which is contributive of one of the oldest definitions of courage: "knowing what is to be feared and what is not to be feared."

To repeat, this knowledge does not eliminate the risks. But it does cut down on what I have called, for lack of a better term, the preventable risks. Such knowledge thus frees us to establish that trust in ourselves and our world which grants to us the play-space in which we can take those risks -- rational risks -- which hold us open to question, which so exhilarate and reward us.

The co-presence of risk, trust, and knowledge in our play suggest the appeal to us of situations which might be characterized as precarious, as up to chance. Indeed as Huizinga has observed in Homo Ludens, the etymology of the word "play" confirms this. The oldest meaning of the Old English word "plegan" from which our word "play" gets derived is "to vouch or stand guarantee for, to take a risk, to expose oneself to danger for someone or something."[17] So we will ski at the very edge of our ability to control our movements -- but with equipment that we trust to be durable and dependable. We will chance winning or losing in a game -- but with opponents whom we trust share our attitude toward the game. And in the intensity and passion of close competition we will risk alienation from our competitors -- but with opponents whom we trust are not out to start a fight from the beginning. The risk-full play situations that we seek, then, seem to be an image of a kind of life which attracts many of us, a life which affirms the appeal of the precarious, but within a context of

135

that trust in our world and knowledge of it which encourages us to face up to that precariousness rather than to flee it. Perhaps it is these elements of trust and knowledge which separate "reasonable" from "unreasonable" risks, and which thus makes our play rational rather than irrational, even and especially in the midst of great risks. In so playing, as I have suggested, we do what is natural, what is founded in our nature. But to repeat an earlier point, we at the same time do what is best for us to do, what points -- however precariously -- toward the telos of human being.

Footnotes, Chapter 6

1). Parts of this chapter have their source in three
earlier papers: "Competition and Friendship",
published in The Journal of the Philosophy of
Sport, vol. V, 1978, and in Sport and the Body,
A Philosophical Symposium, eds. Gerber and
Morgan, 2nd edition, Philadelphia, Lea &
Febiger, 1979: "Living Dangerously" Reflections
on the Risk-Taking Element in Play", presented
at the annual conference of the Philosophical
Society for the Study of Sport, Ft. Worth,
Texas, Fall, 1978: "Playing Dangerously:
Reflections on the Risk-Taking Element in
Sport", presented as the H. Stafford Little
Public Lecture, Princeton University, February
24, 1982.

2). Marx, to take an important example from outside
the sporting domain, is profoundly ambiguous on
the direction of the causal link between
competition and alienation. See his Economic
and Philosophic Manuscripts of 1844, in Karl
Marx: Early Writings, trans. and ed. by
T.B. Bottomore, New York, McGraw-Hill, 1963,
page 131.

3). "Athletics and Angst: Reflections on the
Philosophical Relevance of Play", in Sport and
the Body, A Philosophial Symposium, page 87.

4). Hobbes, Thomas, Leviathan, New York,
Bobbs-Merrill, 1958, pages 87, 106.

5). Hegel, G.W.F., The Phenomenology of Spirit,
trans. A.V. Miller Oxford, Clarendon Press,
1977, pages 113-114.

6). Marx, op. cit. page 131.

7). A view perhaps most easily associated with the
writings of Rousseau, but pervasive today in
both "liberal" and "radical" analyses of
society.

8). Smith, Adam, The Wealth of Nations, New York,
Modern Library, 1937, page 423.

9). Nietzsche, Friedrich, Thus Spoke Zarathustra, in
The Portable Nietzsche, ed. W. Kaufmann, New
York, Viking Press, 1954, pages 168, 190.

10). Marx, op. cit. page 155.

11). Buber, I and Thou, trans. R.G. Smith, New York,
Charles Scribners Sons, 1958, passim.

12). Cf. Kretchmar, Scott, "From Test to Contest: An
Analysis of Two Kinds of Counterpoint in Sport",
Journal of the Philosophy of Sport, vol. II,

1975, pages 23-30.

13). See A. Alvarez, "I like to Risk My Life", in Gerber, Sport and the Body: A Philosophical Symposium, 1st edition, pages 203-205, for an instructive account of some of the considerations involved here.

14). Beisser, Arnold, The Madness in Sport, 2nd edition, Bowie, Maryland, Charles Press, 1977, esp. chapters 3, 5, 6, 14.

15). Alvarez, op. cit. page 204.

16). Ibid.

17). Huizinga, Johan, Homo Ludens, Boston, Beacon Press, 1950, page 39.

Chapter 7: The Play of Philosophy

In Part II, I tried to set out an understanding of what I there called the stance of play as responsive openness which would be true of all play. To make that point, I employed, by and large, examples which were more or less standard: basketball, skiing, football, fishing, playing house. But my refusal to insist that I had therein achieved a "definition" of play, neither too broad nor too narrow, implied what I now wish to develop, that there are many activities, not usually identified with play, which on my understanding could be seen to embody at least playful elements, even if other considerations may lead us finally to hold back from calling them simply instances of play. It strikes me that art, for example, embodies many of the characteristics I associated with play. Who is more responsively open to color than the artist, to sound than the musician, to words than the poet? Similarly, the themes of finitude, of value, and of fun, which I suggested were central to the experience of play, are often present in artistic experience. And to be sure, there is often something playful about art at its highest moments. In this final chapter, however, I wish to consider the playful dimension of another fundamental human possibility, philosophy; this final chapter will thus be in part a reflection on the very act of writing it, and on the book of which it is the conclusion. The Platonic Socrates once suggests that philosophic writing should be understood as the playfulness of intelligent people.[1] I wish to give that playful point serious meaning.

The reader will recall my extended discussion in Part II of how the stance of responsive openness was grounded in a number of dualities in human being: our nature as incomplete yet overfull, as both monadic and rational, and as a vacillation between mastery and submission. The first duality, which strikes me as the deepest and in a way, the ground of the other two, finds perhaps its greatest formulation in the thinking of Plato on eros. Let me now attempt to encapsulate that teaching, particularly as it is presented in Plato's dialogue, the Symposium, without, of course, turning this book into a detailed exegesis of a Platonic dialogue. I shall be concentrating here largely on the speeches of Aristophanes and Socrates, for it is in them that the core of the teaching regarding our ontological status as incomplete and overfull is presented. I will thus present a reformulation of this conception of human nature which makes explicit its origins in the Platonic teaching on eros.

Aristophanes presents only one side of the story. He is especially impressed by the human condition of incompleteness, which he presents in his hilarious and ribald account of the development of human sexuality.² We were once double beings, he says, with two heads, four arms and legs, etc. We came in three varieties: a double male, of which each half was what we now call "male", a double female, each half a female, and an androgynous being, half male and half female. In our double state, we were of course very powerful, but unfortunately, also very arrogant, full of hybris. We tried to overthrow the gods, and therefore had to be punished, the net result of which was that the gods finally decided to split us in two, so that we would be twice in number (to assure more sacrifices) but only half as strong. This splitting of human nature generated the three sexual types, homosexuals, lesbians, and heterosexuals, depending on what sort of whole being was our origin. But it also generated eros, or love. For our immediate reaction to this split state was to try to join together again, and this effort to become whole again out of our incompleteness is called love. Now, Aristophanes, for his own reasons, wants us to think primarily in this account of the actual physical attempt to become whole by joining together, the act of sexual love. But it is not difficult to "demythologize" his account and see that implicit in it is a profound teaching concerning human nature itself. Human beings, first, are "fallen" from an original state. This is the pagan version of original sin. Moreover, the state from which we fell was itself radically defective, characterized by excessive hybris and impiety. Thus the very state toward which we strive to return is itself unsatisfactory. We are not only fallen, but tragically so. The mode of our fallenness is our state of being as incomplete, radically partial. This, upon reflection, has three "moments", with which we will be familiar from an earlier context. The first we can call the ontological moment. We are as incomplete; that is now our very nature. Eros is our nature, not just a contingent attribute. Second, we recognize or experience that incompleteness. Rocks may be incomplete, but they are not erotic because they do not experience their incompleteness. Third,

140

eros is the desire, the impetus, to overcome that experienced incompleteness, to achieve a (original) state of completeness or wholeness. What we call "love" is obviously one manifestation of our erotic nature, and it is the one Aristophanes wants us to think of. But as Socrates' speech makes clear, there are other manifestations of this erotic status. In principle, any exhibition of this triadic structure of incompleteness, experience thereof, and striving to overcome it is in fact an exhibition of our nature as erotic. This is really, albeit implicitly, an account of all human aspiration, human pro-jection. I may, for example, experience an incompleteness of political power, and run for public office as an effort to overcome it, or experience an incompleteness of wealth, and seek a fortune, or, decisively for Socrates (but problematically for Aristophanes) I may experience an incompleteness of wisdom, and strive to overcome it; I may become a philosopher. This, parenthetically, is our first sign of the erotic nature of philosophy.

Now in less mythological form, Socrates, speaking in behalf of the priestess Diotima, accepts Aristophanes teaching on eros as human nature, but accepts it as only half the story. We get our first clue to the imcompleteness of Aristophanes' own account when Socrates, speaking in behalf of Diotima, relates the mythical parentage of eros.[3] Eros, to be sure, is the child of Penia, Want or Poverty. This represents the dimension of incompleteness of which Aristophanes spoke. But eros has heterosexual parentage, unlike the "heavenly eros" of Pausanias' speech. Its father is Poros, Plenty, Resourcefulness. This is the element in our erotic nature that Aristophanes missed, and which makes his own account partial and too pessimistic. Eros, which shares in the nature of both parents, is both incomplete and overfull. Its overfullness, plenty, or resourcefulness is the source of its "power of activity", of the energy which flows out of us toward the world, which impels us to the world and which the world receives from us; it is literally the ex-pression of ourselves, the gift of our fullness. Consequently, says Socrates, all humans are "pregnant", an apt metaphor for our fullness and capacity for overflowing and ex-pression. This dimension of our eros, we are told, is the source of all our creativity, from the generation of physical children to the creation of laws, poems, and works of

141

art.[4] Not just our yearning striving to overcome incompleteness but our creative fullness as well arises out of, and so is grounded in, our nature as erotic. It is fair to say, then, that the word Plato uses for this aspect of our nature, this "unity of difference" of incompleteness and overfullness, is eros.

At least one important consequence of this position has to do with an issue discussed as early as chapter 2, that of so-called dualism. Recall that it was observed there that, phenomenologically, our play experience seems to be that of a unity of our power of activity, a unity which was in clear tension with the dualism of mind or soul and body which we often assert on philosophical or religious grounds. Plato, as most are aware, is often regarded as such a dualist, largely in my view due to a misinterpretation of dialogues such as the Phaedo. The teaching on eros entails a different view, one altogether compatible with our experience of play. Our eros, we now see, gets manifested in manifold ways. Some of those ways are primarily bodily: sexuality, some might say, or most of our sports. Others are more predominantly "soulful": poetry, or "spiritual" love, or philosophy. In this context, one may indeed speak, as Socrates does, of "soul" and "body". But this is no longer the language of substantial dualism. "Soul" and "body" are not here two distinct substances whose unity is either opaque or non-existent. They are rather two different manifestations of a unity, the unity which is our eros. The play experience, an experience of that unified immersion in which our involvement is total, is thus an experience which cuts through the superficial duality of our bodily and spiritual expressions to their unity in our natures as erotic.

It is now possible to state more clearly how the other two dualities, monadic/relational and mastery/submission, are related to our nature as incomplete and overfull which we can now call our eros. On the one hand, eros makes us relational. Because we are incomplete, because we do not have the ingredients of completeness within ourselves, our yearning for wholeness forces us toward that which is other than us in our quest for wholeness: the world and other people. We are thus "by nature" relational in the sense that our impetus to "be-toward-the-world" and to "be-toward-others" is a function of our eros.

On the other hand, the specific ways in which we manifest our eros make us the unique individuals that we are. To use previous examples, if I am a husband, father, teacher, philosopher, and athlete, these are the ways in which I have experienced incompleteness and tried to overcome it: they are also the ways in which I have "poured myself forth" to the world in my fullness. My eros thus individualizes me as the unique individual that I am. To paraphrase Heidegger, eros is in each case mine. Moreover, that dimension of my eros which is my fullness and overflowing capacity grants to me that autonomy, that independence, which constitutes my monadic aspect. To sum this up, we can say that eros individualizes us in our monadic nature, but it individualizes us as relational.

We can reiterate in a similar way the connection of eros to our propensity to take the stances of dominance and submission. Insofar as we are more moved by our incompleteness, and perhaps forgetful of our power of activity, we from time to time see our places as accepting the way we are and the way things are; we take the stance of submission and see it as natural to do so. But in so far as we exhilarate in our fullness and power of activity, perhaps forgetting our partiality, we take the stance of dominance and consider it, too, as natural. Both stances are natural, but both defective because both only partial expressions of our natures as erotic in the full sense.

We can now relate these considerations more specifically to play. The stance of responsive openness, insofar as it is grounded in these three dualities and especially in the first, is grounded in our erotic natures. Our openness towards the world and its possibilities is grounded in and necessitated by our ontological status as incomplete. If we were not incomplete, we would not be called upon to be open to possibilities of fulfillment. There is a wonderful portrayal of this point in the Sumerian epic, The Myth of Gilgamesh. Gilgamesh, vividly, even painfully aware of his incompleteness, focuses especially on his temporal incompleteness; he is finite, he will not live forever, and he knows it. However, he has heard of a person, the only human ever to be made immortal, Utnapishtim, whom he decides to seek out in order to discover his wisdom. When, after a long and arduous journey, he finally meets Utnapishtim, he is crushed with disappointment; he laments,

> "I look at you now, Utnapishtim, and
> your appearance is no different from
> mine; there is nothing strange in your
> features. I thought I should find you
> like a hero prepared for battle, but
> you lie here taking your ease on your
> back."[5].

Gilgamesh´s disappointment, we might say, is a consequence of his failure to appreciate the positive value of incompleteness, or at least its consolation. Only because we are incomplete are we open toward things, are we called upon to be vividly aware of the possibilities presented to us.

Conversely, the responsive dimension in the stance of play is founded in that other side of eros, our overfullness or "plenty". Because our eros is also overflowing power of activity, we are not merely incomplete in the sense of emptiness or impotence. Our fullness makes us _responsive_ to our situation, to the possibilities presented to us in our incompleteness. Clearly, the stance of responsive openness is grounded in our eros, and, it is worth noting, this grounding is teleological. Because of our erotic natures, responsive openness becomes not merely descriptive of what we are but a _desideratum_. The best that we can be, the way we can best fulfill our natures, and so the _telos_ of human being, is to be as responsively open. From this, and insofar as the stance of responsive openness is characteristic of play, two important consequences follow. First, we play because we are erotic; play arises out of our very natures as incomplete and overfull. But second, play is also a _telos_ of human being. One of the best, the highest of human possibilities is play. What Schiller says is true: we are most truly human -- in the teleological sense -- when we play.[6]

The next step in the development of the connection of play and philosophy is to remind the reader of the relation, briefly discussed in an earlier chapter, between responsive openness, eros, and questioning. Let us begin first by showing the connection between questioning and eros. To question, to hold anything open to question, and more generally to take a questioning stance toward the world, is at

144

once to testify to our erotic nature. To question is to recognize and admit incompleteness. We question because we do not know, because we experience an incompleteness of knowledge. Yet to question is at once to respond to that incompleteness. If we were merely incomplete, we would simply acknowledge our lack of knowledge and leave it at that; we would accept our ignorance. But questioning is a refusal to do so. Infused as well with overfullness and power of activity, we do not merely accept our incompleteness but move to overcome it. We question, and in so doing, again, testify to our incompleteness and our overfullness, and so to our eros.

The connection between questioning and responsive openness should be equally clear. To question is to be open to things. We speak of "holding things open to question", and we refer to people who refuse to question things as "close-minded". Questioning thus is an exhibition of the stance of openness. But just as evidently, questioning is not a passive openness which merely accepts; it is a responsive openness which responds to the openness in and by questioning. The stance of questioning is thus a paradigm of that "unity within difference" which is responsive openness. Grounded in eros, questioning exhibits our natures as such and at the same time calls for and manifests responsive openness. The question now arises whether there might not be a connection between the stance of questioning, philosophy, and play.

Certainly the connection could not be shown by appealing to many versions of philosophy, especially many contemporary ones, which have little enough to do with either questioning or play. Instead, I shall cite and briefly develop a conception of philosophy which I would espouse but which I am by no means the first to espouse. It is a conception first articulated and exhibited by the Platonic Socrates. It is not only consistent with but called for by the recognition of human nature as erotic. One locus of that articulation is in Plato's Apology. Let me summarize the position as follows.

Central to Socrates' defense of himself and philosophy in the Apology is his effort to overcome the contention that he, like the sophists, considers himself to be wise. Quite to the contrary, Socrates almost exaggerates the force with which he is aware of his lack of wisdom.[7] He knows, above all, that he is not wise. Nevertheless, he continues, the problem is more complex, for the oracle at Delphi, speaking in the name of the god and therefore necssarily speaking the truth, has said that no one is wiser than Socrates. Socrates is faced with a riddle; how can it be that no one is wiser than him, if he knows that he is not wise? Socrates procedes to relate the tale of how he, in an effort to resolve this riddle, went to a series of reputed wise people -- sophists, statesmen, poets -- to question them in the hopes of discovering their wisdom and thereby "refuting" the oracle's claim that he is the wisest of men. Quite to the contrary, what he discovers upon questioning these people is that although they certainly claimed to be wise and thought that they were wise they really were not. Socrates concludes that in a curious way, the oracle was right. He is wiser than other people, but just on this point, that he, not being wise, does not think that he is wise, whereas most other people, and certainly the reputed wise people whom he questioned, thought that they were wise, although in fact they were not. [8] Socrates' wisdom, it is important to note, is thus <u>self-knowledge</u> in this sense: knowing what he knows and what he does not know.

Immediately we can note that there is something altogether extraordinary about Socrates' wisdom and his self-knowledge. We usually think of wisdom as a form of knowledge in the straightforward sense whose fundamental mode of expression is assertion. That is, the wise person is someone who knows certain things, and the way that he or she exhibits that wisdom is by asserting it, by relating to us, even proving, the wisdom. Consequent upon this understanding, self-knowledge in the usual sense is also taken to be assertive. If I am a person of self-knowledge, then I know a number of truths about myself which I am capable of articulating and documenting. But Socrates denies that his wisdom is of this sort: consequently, his self-knowledge is different as well. Socrates' wisdom is not a massive body of knowledge which he can dispense, but his recognition of his lack of wisdom. How does this wisdom get exhibited? By the endless repetition of the statement that he knows that he lacks wisdom? That would be vacuous wisdom indeed. Socrates' exhibits his wisdom -- his recognition of his lack -- by <u>questioning</u>. It is important to appreciate this difficult point. Socrates has a certain wisdom, a certain knowledge, which is best exhibited not by assertion but by questioning. For

146

questioning does indeed, in the very act of questioning, testify to the recognition on the part of the questioner of the lack of wisdom and consequent desire to overcome it. Contrary to our usual presumption that questioning exhibits merely a lack of knowledge and that it is assertion through which genuine knowlede is exhibited, Socrates shows us that questioning, or at least certain modes of questioning, is founded upon and an exhibition of knowledge. What knowledge? Self-knowledge, understood again as knowing what I know and what I do not know. Let us restate the situation in terms of Socrates' understanding of self-knowledge. Usually we think of self-knowledge in the usual sense of knowing a number of truths about myself which I can articulate and support ("I am slightly neurotic, I am afraid of heights, I have to work hard to control my temper," etc.). On this view, Socrates' self-knowledge as knowing what he knows and what he does not know would be exhibited by, presumably, a rather long two-column list, headed, respectively, "what I know" and "what I do not know". Does Socrates ever so much as hint that this is what he has in mind? Never. But Socrates does indeed exhibit his self-knowledge, his recognition of what he knows and what he does not know. How? Again, through his questioning. I reiterate this initially strange point: the way to reveal certain kinds of knowledge, specifically self-knowledge, is through questioning. Questioning once again is shown to be not empty or groundless but founded on and an exhibition of knowledge, self-knowledge.[9].

Socrates is famous for the consistency with which he carried out this self-understanding. Throughout the Platonic dialogues, we see him avoiding claims to assertable knowledge, insisting that he does not know about the subject of discussion, and instead taking a stance of questioning. When Socrates is told of an understanding of what friendship is, or what sophrosyne is, or what piety is, he neither accepts it not counters it with his own "theory". Instead, he questions it, openly and responsively, we might say. But what is this procedure of questioning, this stance that Socrates takes again and again toward all views? It is nothing else than philosophy itself, at least as Socrates understood it. Philosophy, that is -- contrary to most modern understandings -- is not fundamentally assertive, the positing and proving of "theories" about this or that, but interrogative, the

147

taking again and again of the stance of questioning toward things. By recalling the literal meaning of the term "philosophy", we can see how well-founded Socrates' view is in terms of his own understanding of human being.

"Philo-sophia" means, literally, the "love of wisdom". It is therefore founded in our natures as erotic. This means, as Socrates makes clear in the Symposium, that to love wisdom signifies already that one lacks it, recognizes that lack, and strives to overcome it, that is, seeks to become wise. In short, philosophy is a manifestation of eros, in Socrates' view the highest manifestation. The philosophic stance of questioning, arising out of the recognition of our lack of wisdom (which Socrates calls aporia) and consequent striving to overcome it, has, however, the greatest degree of self-consciousness of any of the manifestations of eros. Philosophy is erotic, knows itself to be so, and has as the object of its fulfillment the highest of objects: wisdom. As such, it is the telos of our erotic natures. Once again in the teleological sense, philosophy is both natural to human being and our highest possibility.

From this construal of eros and the conception of philosophy it founds, we can derive an understanding of rationality which should help us respond to the charge that play is fundamentally irrational, a charge we have documented both among well-known philosophers and in the lay understanding of play. One of the least controversial statements one might make about the Platonic dialogues is that in them Socrates stands forth as a champion of rationality. But how is that rationality exhibited? By asserting a number of "theses" or "theories" which Socrates goes on to "prove"? Hardly. Socrates' questioning stance and his pursuit of philosophy as a holding open to question of things suggests that philosophic rationality cannot be reduced to asserting only theses which one can prove, or demonstrating again and again the "causal nexus" within which a given theory or fact is to be founded (although it might include such considerations). More fundamental to what we might call Socratic rationality is the willingness and ability continually to hold one's views and oneself open to question. Perhaps the most famous line in the Apology is Socrates' remark that "the unexamined life is not worth living."[10] He does not say, "the unproved thesis is not worth asserting". The

rationality of philosophy is most fundamentally
founded therefore in the stance of questioning, which
in turn is founded in our natures as erotic.
Rationality, so understood, is thus <u>natural</u> to human
being. It is worth noting that irrationality on this
view would have as its paradigm not "saying things one
can't prove" or participating in actions without
knowing the relevant "causal nexus", but the refusal
to hold one's standpoint open to question. The height
of irrationality, from the Socratic standpoint, is
close-mindedness, or fanaticism.

We can now relate this to the question of the
rationality of play. We have already developed the
kinship between play and philosophy insofar as both
are characterized in their nature by responsive
openness. In turn, that responsive openness was
related to the stance of questioning, whether that
questioning take the form of the explicit questioning
of oneself, typical of philosophy, or the less verbal
calling oneself into question exhibited in play. In
turn, questioning, play, and philosophy were seen to
be founded in our natures as erotic. If, then, play
as responsive openness is itself a mode of the stance
of questioning, and if the nurturing of that
interrogative stance is paradigmatic of rationality,
should we continue to speak of the irrationality of
play or not rather recognize in play an exhibition of
what is quite literally (and teleologically) our
<u>natural</u> rationality? Of those thinkers who assert the
irrationality of play, whether because its causes
cannot be discovered, or its risks justified by
proofs, we can ask, is it that play is irrational or
rather that the conception of rationality under which
the charge is made is inadequate?

Play and philosophy are rational, albeit rational
in a sense always founded in their literal
questionability. As questionable, however, there is
always and inevitably something precarious about them.
The questionability of Socratic philosophy will never
have as its beginning or end the "point of indubitable
certitude" asserted by Descartes,[11] and the risks of
play will never appeal to those of us who seek most of
all security (or perhaps, to all of us when we are in
those moods which seek security).

Philosophy is thus, like play to which it is
akin, a good, but precariously so. Founded as both
are in our nature as erotic, they both have the

149

character always of possibility, as something always
outstanding, not completed. This is a mode of their
finitude and means that both can as often fail as
succeed, can be a danger as well as the highest of
blessings. To recognize our nature as erotic is to
recognize human life as inherently unstable, unstable
by its incompleteness, unstable by its constant
yearning for and active striving for completeness. As
incomplete and therefore finite, human life will also
necessarily be shot through with error and failure.
Our efforts to move toward completeness, and that
means especially for us our philosophizing and our
play, are both therefore bound to fail as often as
succeed, and in a way finally to fail altogether.
There is something tragic about human being. We have
developed myriad ways to overlook, to hide, to deny,
this tragic character, this finitude, this
precariousness. But there are also certain modes of
activity, certain ways of being, which face up to our
nature, affirm it, celebrate it. Play is one such
way, and philosophy. To cite one more time the
example of the Platonic Socrates, he shows us that it
is possible to recognize all this, and be happy.
Socrates demonstrates this perhaps most obviously by
the sometimes startling fact that he regularly seems
to be happy, even when he is in jail and on the day of
his death. But the point is made in a subtler and
deeper way by a curious incident in Plato's Apology.
There, Socrates, having been found guilty of impiety
and corrupting the youth and sentenced to death,
explains why he does not fear death. He does not
know, he says, whether death is a great evil or a
great good.[12] But to fear death would be to assume
that it is an evil, and therefore would be an instance
of "thinking I know what I in fact do not know", a
state which Socrates has just prided himself on
avoiding. Therefore he does not fear death. Now a
moment's reflection will show that there is something
wonderfully naive about Socrates' words. He acts as
if the only thing people feared were things that we
know to be evil. He thus leaves out of consideration
what is perhaps the greatest object of fear among
humans: fear of the unknown. It is almost as if it
does not occur to Socrates that one might fear the
unknown. To put the point more positively, Socrates
conducts himself in such a way that he does not fear
but affirms, welcomes, the unknown. And that way is
the way of philosophy, understood as a stance of
questioning. For to question, as we have seen, is
neither to flee from nor deny the unknown, but to

150

affirm it as one's way, as one's home. As Henry Bugbee once put it, our true home is wilderness, even the world of everyday.[13]

To make one's home the wilderness is to affirm human life as what it is, precarious, finite, unknown. I cannot repeat the point too often that we have developed myriad ways to deny this, to flee it. Often when we do think of affirming it, we do so in a mood of __Angst__, with our teeth gritted and our fists clenched. But what Socratic philosophy shows us is that it is also possible to face up to this recognition and to live it out with integrity, in happiness.

But Socratic philosophy, in so far as it exhibits responsive openness, the recognition of finitude, of the issue of value, and yes, of fun, can be a mode of play, and perhaps one of its highest manifestations. To the extent, then, that I have shown the kinship of philosophy and play, I have meant to suggest that an affirmation of precariousness and finitude does not exclude but celebrates play as at the pinnacle of human possibilities. In play, too, we know ourselves, we are ourselves.

1). Plato, Phaedrus, 276d.
2). Plato, Symposium, 189c-193d. The following is a discussion of the gist of the entire speech.
3). Ibid, 203b ff.
4). Ibid, 206c-209c.
5). The Epic of Gilgamesh, trans. N.K. Sandars, Baltimore, Penguin Books, 1964, page 104.
6). Schiller, Friedrich, On the Aesthetic Education of Man, trans. R. Snell, New York, Frederick Ungar Publishing Co., 1965, page 80.
7). Plato, Apology, 19 ff.
8). Ibid, 23 ff.
9). For an extended discussion of this point, see my The Virtue of Philosophy: An Interpretation of Plato's Charmides, Athens, Ohio, Ohio University Press, 1981, especially chapters 6-9.
10). Plato, Apology, 38a.
11). Descartes, Rene, Meditations on First Philosophy, in Philosophical Works of Descartes, vol. 1, trans. Haldane & Ross, Cambridge, Cambridge University Press, 1931, "Meditation II", page 149.
12). Plato, Apology, 29a.
13). Bugbee, Henry, Inward Morning, New York, Collier Books, 1961, page 83.

References

Allison, David. "Derrida and Wittgenstein: Playing the Game." Research in Phenomenology. Volume VIII, 1978.

Alvarez, A. "I Like to Risk My Life" in Gerber, Ellen (Editor), Sport and The Body: A Philosophical Symposium. First Edition. Philadelphia: Lea & Febiger, 1972.

Bacon, Francis. "Instauratio Magna" in Philosophical Works. Edited by J.M. Robertson. New York: E.P. Dutton, 1905.

Bacon, Francis. Novum Organum.

Beisser, Arnold. The Madness in Sport. Second Edition. Bowie, Md.: Charles Press Publishers, 1977.

Belaief, Lynn. "Meanings of the Body". Journal of the Philosophy of Sport. Volume 4, 1977.

Boss, G. "Jeu et Philosophie". Revue de Metaphysique et de Morale. Volume 84, number 4, October-December, 1979.

Brohm, Jean-Marie. Sport: A Prison of Measured Time. Translated by Ion Fraser. London: Ink Links Press, 1978.

Buber, Martin. I And Thou. Translated by Ronald Gregor Smith. New York: Charles Scribner's Sons, 1958.

Bugbee, Henry. Inward Morning. New York: Collier Books, 1961.

Camus, Albert. Resistance, Rebellion, and Death. New York: Alfred Knopf, 1961.

Caputo, John. "Being, Ground and Play in Heidegger". Man and World. Volume 3, 1971.

Caputo, John. The Mystical Element in Heidegger's Thought. Athens, Ohio: Ohio University Press, 1978.

Derrida, Jacques. L'ecriture et la Difference.
Paris, 1967. Translated by Alan Bass as Writing and
Difference. Chicago: University of Chicago Press,
1978.

Derrida, Jacques. Of Grammatology. Translated by
Gayatri Chakravorty Spivak. Baltimore: Johns Hopkins
University Press, 1976.

Derrida, Jacques. Speech and Phenomena. Translated
by David Allison. Evanston: Northwestern University
Press, 1973.

Descartes, Rene. Meditationes de Prima Philosophia.
Paris: Librairie Philosophique de J. Vrin, 1960.

Descartes, Rene. Meditations On First Philosophy. In
Philosophical Works of Descartes. Volume I.
Translated by Haldane & Ross. Cambridge, Cambridge
University Press, 1931.

Feezell, Rudolph. "Play, Freedom, and Sport".
Philosophy Today. Volume 25. Summer, 1981.

Fink, Eugen. Nietzsches Philosophie. Stuttgart:
Kohlhammer, 1968.

Fink, Eugen. Oase des Glucks: Gedanken zu einer
Ontologie des Spiels. Freiburg: Alber-Verlag, 1960.

Fink, Eugen. Spiel als Weltsymbol. Stuttgart:
Kohlhammer Verlag, 1960.

Fink, Eugen. "The Ontology of Play". In Sport and
the Body: A Philosophical Symposium. Edited by Ellen
Gerber and Wm. Morgan. Philadelphia: Lea & Febiger,
1979.

Foucault, Michel. "Nietzsche, Geneology, History".
In Language, Counter-Memory Practice: Selected Essays
and Interviews. Translated and Edited by Donald
Bouchard and Sherry Simon. Ithaca: Cornell
University Press, 1977.

Foucault, Michel. The Archaelogy of Knowledge.
Translated by A.M.S. Smith. New York: Harper
Colophon Books, 1972.

Foucault, Michel. The Order of Things. New York:
Pantheon Books, 1970.

Gadamer, Hans-Georg. _Truth and Method_. Translated by
Garrett Barden and John Cumming. New York:
Continuum, 1975.

Galileo. _Opere Complete di Galileo Galilei_. Firenze:
1842.

Gerber, Ellen, and Morgan, Wm. (Editors). _Sport and
the Body: A Philosophical Symposium_. Second Edition.
Philadelphia: Lea & Febiger, 1979.

Gibran, Kahlil. _The Prophet_. New York: Knopf, 1966.

Gilbert, Wm. and Williamson, Nancy. "Sport Is Unfair
to Women". _Sports Illustrated_. May 28, 1973.

Guttman, Allen. _From Ritual to Record: The Nature of
Modern Sports_. New York: Columbia University Press,
1978.

Hans, James S. _The Play of the World_. Amherst:
University of Massachusetts Press, 1981.

Hegel, G.W.F. _The Phenomenology of Spirit_.
Translated by A.V. Miller. Oxford: Clarendon Press,
1977.

Heidegger, Martin. _Being and Time_. Translated by
Marquarrie and Robinson. New York: Harper & Row,
1962.

Heidegger, Martin. _Der Satz vom Grund_. Neske, 1957.

Heidegger, Martin. _Identity and Difference_.
Translated by Joan Stambaugh. New York: Harper
Torchbooks, 1969.

Heidegger, Martin. "Language". In _Poetry,
Language,Thought_. Translated by Albert Hofstadter.
New York: Harper & Row, 1971.

Heidegger, Martin. _Nietzsche I_. Pfullingen:
G. Neske Verlag, 1961.

Heidegger, Martin. "The Origin of a Work of Art". In
Poetry, Language, Thought. Translated by Albert
Hofstadter. New York: Harper & Row, 1971.

Heidegger, Martin. What is Called Thinking?
Translated by Fred Wieck and Glenn Gray. New York:
Harper & Row, 1968.

Heraclitus. "Fragment 52". In Die Fragmente der
Vorsokratiker. Edited by Diels and Kranz. Zurich:
Weidmann, 1968.

Herrigel, Eugen. Zen In the Art of Archery. New
York: Vintage Books, 1971.

Hobbes, Thomas. Leviathan. New York: Bobbs-Merrill,
1958.

Hoch, Paul. Rip Off the Big Game: The Exploitation
of Sports by the Power Elite. New York: Anchor
Books, 1972.

Huizinga, Johan. Homo Ludens: A Study of the Play
Element in Culture. Boston: Beacon Press, 1950.

Hyland, Drew. "Athletics and Angst: Reflections on
the Philosophical Relevance of Play". In Sport and
the Body: A Philosophical Symposium. Second Edition.
Edited by Ellen Gerber & Wm. Morgan. Philadelphia:
Lea & Febiger, 1979.

Hyland, Drew. "Competition and Friendship". The
Journal of the Philosophy of Sport. Volume 5, 1978.

Hyland, Drew. "Playing Dangerously: Reflections on
the Risk-Taking Element in Sport". Presented as the
H. Stafford Little Public Lecture, Princeton
University, February 24, 1982.

Hyland, Drew. The Virtue of Philosophy: An
Interpretation of Plato's Charmides. Athens, Ohio:
Ohio University Press, 1981.

Janicaud, Dominique. "Presence and Appropriation:
Derrida and the Question of the Overcoming of
Metaphysical Language". Research in Phenomenology.
Volume VIII, 1978.

Kant, Immanuel. Critique of Pure Reason. Translated
by N.K. Smith. London: McMillan & Co., 1961.

Kant, Immanuel. Idea For a Universal History With a
Cosmopolitan Intent. In The Philosophy of Kant.
Edited by Carl Frederick. New York: The Modern
Library, 1949.

Keating, James. Competition and Playful Activities.
Washington, D.C.: University Press of America, 1978.

Kierkegaard, Soren. Concluding Unscientific
Postscript. Translated by David Swenson. Princeton:
Princeton University Press, 1941.

Kierkegaard, Soren. Philosophical Fragments.
Translated by David Swenson. Princeton: Princeton
University Press, 1936.

Kierkegaard, Soren. The Journals of Kierkegaard.
Edited by Alexander Dru. New York: Harper & Row,
1958.

Kretchmar, Scott. "From Test to Contest: An Analysis
of Two Kinds of Counterpoint in Sport". Journal of
the Philosophy of Sport. Volume 2, 1975.

Leonard, George. The Ultimate Athlete. New York:
Viking Press, 1974.

Machiavelli, Niccolo. The Prince and Other
Discourses. New York: Modern Library, 1950.

Marx, Karl. Economic and Philosophic Manuscripts of
1844. In Karl Marx: Early Writings. Translated by
T.B. Bottomore. New York: McGraw-Hill, 1963.

Marx, Karl. On the Jewish Question. In Karl Marx:
Early Writings. Translated and Edited by
T.B. Bottomore. New York: McGraw-Hill, 1963.

Marx, Karl. "Theses on Feuerbach". In The German
Ideology. Edited by C.J. Arthur. New York:
International Publishers, 1970.

McBride, Frank. "Toward a Non-Definition of Sport".
Journal of the Philosophy of Sport. Volume II, 1975.

Miller, J. Hillis. "The Disarticulation of the Self
in Nietzsche". Monist. Volume 64, number 2, April,
1981.

Morgan, Wm., "Play, Utopia, Dystopia: Prologue to a
Ludic Theory of the State". Unpublished paper.

Nietzsche, Friedrich. The Birth of Tragedy.
Translated by Walter Kaufmann. New York: Vintage
Books, 1967.

Nietzsche, Friedrich. The Will to Power. Translated
by Kaufmann and Hollingdale. New York: Random House,
1967.

Nietzsche, Friedrich. Thus Spoke Zarathustra. In The
Portable Nietzsche. Edited by Walter Kaufmann. New
York: Viking Press, 1954.

Novak, Michael. The Joy of Sports. New York: Basic
Books, 1976.

Plato. Apology. In Platonis Opere. Edited by John
Burnet. Oxford: Oxford University Press, 1958.

Plato. Laws. In Platonis Opere. Edited by John
Burnet. Oxford: Oxford University Press, 1958.

Plato. Phaedrus. In Platonis Opere. Edited by John
Burnet. Oxford: Oxford University Press, 1958.

Plato. Symposium. In Platonis Opere. Edited by John
Burnet. Oxford: Oxford University Press, 1958.

Ravizza, Kenneth. "A Study of the Peak Experience in
Sport". Unpublished paper.

Roochnik, David. "Competing Paradigms of Play".
Unpublished paper.

Sage, George (Editor). Sport and American Society.
Second Edition. Reading, Mass.: Addison-Wesley,
1974.

Sandars, S.K. (Editor). The Epic of Gilgamesh.
Baltimore: Penguin Books, 1964.

Sartre, Jean-Paul. Essays in Aesthetics. Translated
by Wade Baskin. New York: Washington Square Press,
1966.

Schiller, Friedrich. On the Aesthetic Education of
Man, in a Series of Letters. Translated by Reginald
Snell. New York: Frederick Ungar Publishing Co.,
1965.

Schurmann, Reiner. "The Ontological Difference and
Political Philosophy". Philosophy and
Phenomenological Research. Volume XL, number 1,
September, 1979.

Scott, Jack. The Athletic Revolution. New York: The
Free Press, 1971.

Silverman, Hugh. "Self-Decentering: Derrida
Incorporated". Research in Phenomenology. Volume
VIII, 1978.

Smith, Adam. The Wealth of Nations. New York:
Modern Library, 1937.

Suits, Bernard. The Grasshopper: Games. Life,
Utopia. Toronto: University of Toronto Press, 1978.

Time Magazine. June 26, 1978.

Vico, G.B. On the Most Ancient Wisdom of the
Italians.

Winnicott, D.W. Playing and Reality. New York:
Basic Books, 1971.

Wolcott, James. "Dust of Snow". Unpublished paper.

INDEX

Professor Drew A. Hyland is Charles A. Dana Professor of Philosophy at Trinity College, Hartford, Connecticut. He has taught and published widely in the history of philosophy, concentrating on Greek Philosophy and 19th and 20th Century Continental Philosophy. In addition, he has published numerous articles in the philosophy of sport, and is past-president of the Philosophical Society for the Study of Sport. His two previous books are The Origins of Philosophy: Its Rise in Myth and The Pre-Socratics, and The Virtue of Philosophy: An Interpretation of Plato's Charmides.